Burying White Privilege

BURYING WHITE PRIVILEGE

Resurrecting a Badass Christianity

Miguel A. De La Torre

WILLIAM B. EERDMANS PUBLISHING COMPANY
GRAND RAPIDS, MICHIGAN

Wm. B. Eerdmans Publishing Co.
4035 Park East Court SE, Grand Rapids, Michigan 49546
www.eerdmans.com

28 27 26 25 24 23 22 21 20 19   1 2 3 4 5 6 7 8 9 10

ISBN 978-0-8028-7688-1

Library of Congress Cataloging-in-Publication Data

A catalog record for this book is available from the Library of Congress

To my *alma mater*

Southern Baptist Theological Seminary

Contents

Preface

Those of us who write seldom realize the influence, if any, our words might have upon the lives of others. Will our words be celebrated or condemned? Will our writing contribute to the discourse or have a negative impact? At times, I write something that I think is brilliant, only to have it be ignored. At other times, I write what I think will fall flat, only to see it go viral. This is what occurred with a short opinion piece that was published on November 13, 2017, on the *Baptist News Global* website. Frankly, I did not consider the op-ed to be one of my better works; nevertheless, it seemed to have hit a nerve. "The Death of Christianity in the US" was shared on social media over 416,000 times. Millions read and commented on the 759-word essay. I was truly taken aback. Ironically, I wrote this particular opinion piece six months earlier and placed it in a file to be quickly forgotten, only to rediscover the piece in November and submit it then for publication.

PREFACE

During an academic conference that same month, Trevor Thompson, acquisitions editor at Wm. B. Eerdmans Publishing Company, approached me and asked if I would consider turning this short piece into a book. I found the proposition intriguing. If I took on this project, my hope was to channel the literary style of my intellectual mentor: the nineteenth-century revolutionary, José Martí. I did not necessarily want to write another academic tome but instead wanted my words to appear as if they were coming from the heart—for they were. If I were to undertake this project, I wanted to engage in a difficult conversation based on my pain, my disillusions, and my hopelessness—a prevailing mood I detect within our society, especially among communities of color. My hope was to disengage the filters and be as real as possible.

Once I decided to write the book, I went to straight to work, placing other pressing projects on hold. It took me thirty-two days (a record for me), writing day and night, to finish the manuscript that you now hold as a book in your hands. Unlike my previous publications, this book exposes my soul and heart to the reader, hence opening myself to become more vulnerable. I have no doubt some might be tempted to demonize me for what I wrote; but I ask, please read my words with an open mind and heart. You need not agree with me, but please listen to how I, and many others who are disenfranchised, feel. I share these painful truths in the hope Christians might discover their own salvation and society might move toward a real rather than illusionary reconciliation. Liberation begins when the marginalized define themselves and their social location. For sixty years, I had been so accustomed to seeing through Eurocentric eyes that it had become second nature. This book represents the therapeutic process of decolonizing my mind, a process of moving away from how I have been taught to see myself, my community, and the overall social order.

Upon finishing the book, I shared the manuscript with my beloved and my children, who provided useful critiques and insights. To them I am grateful not just for their contributions to this work but for all they have contributed to my life and my worldview. I am also grateful to my editor, Trevor, for suggesting the idea for the book, offering me a contract to write, and for providing his many suggestions during the writing and editorial process. His encouragement and support were, and continue to be, greatly appreciated. And finally, I am grateful to you, the reader. I celebrate your courage and patience, especially if you are white, for attempting to see reality through the eyes of those who reside on society's underside. Such a practice needs to be recognized and encouraged. Let us together hope and pray that the humble words found on these pages might lead us all to a deeper and more profound conversation for the good of all our people and our nation.

Let the Dead Bury the Dead

Contrary to stereotypes, millennials and Generation Z are neither self-absorbed nor indifferent to the suffering of the world.[1] These generations, generally speaking, abhor hypocrisy and have a deep grasp of right and wrong. The younger generations express genuine concern for the ever-increasing degradation of the environment and the worsening economy, which prevents so many from becoming self-sufficient adults. Meanwhile, far too many baby boomers sit idly by, ready to offer only their critiques. Our nation's churches could bring forth a powerful word for such a time as this but have instead become convalescent congregations comprised of rapidly shrinking numbers of communicants representing the upper echelons of United States demographics. Not surprisingly, churches have become bastions of indifference and fortresses of the noncommittal.

Lacking vision, churches perish. Millennials are abandoning the church in droves, not because they lack spirituality but because the church has failed them. A 2018 study by the Pew Research Center shows that a higher percentage of millennials categorize themselves as "nones" (36 percent) than as evangelicals (19 percent), mainline (11 percent), or Catholic (16 percent).[2] Why? I suspect many millennials have a deep grasp of justice and an abhorrence for religious institutions that historically justify oppression—economic oppression, racial oppression, gender oppression, and sexual oppression. According to a 2018 study, 31 percent of millennials and 23 percent of Generation Z reject Christianity in any form because they are repelled by the hypocrisy of Christians.[3] They recognize you cannot love the God whom you cannot see while hating your gay neighbor, your "illegal" neighbor, or your Muslim neighbor whom you can see. Not surprisingly, members of Generation Z increasingly embrace atheism at a staggering pace. This move away from the church is not limited to the young, those coming of age during the new millennium. According to a 2017 study by the Pew Research Center, 27 percent of the overall population claims to be "spiritual but not religious," while another 18 percent state they are "neither religious nor spiritual." Less than half of the people in this so-called Christian nation (48 percent) would characterize themselves as "religious and spiritual."[4]

The death of Christianity within the United States has been a slow process, and it may very well be in its final throes. So I say, let the dead bury their dead.

This next generation, which will soon be inheriting the power structures of the United States, recognizes that the barbarians are not at the gate. The barbarians are and always have been the gatekeepers. The next generation gets it! And while some millennials and those of Generation Z can find common ground with the good news, they are turned off by money-grubbing clergy who stand in solidarity with silence and are too fearful of offending the wealthy, older, tithing congregants responsible for their compensation. In the graveyard where Eurocentric doctrines have gone to perish, and where churches act as catacombs and seminaries become cemeteries, cathedrals stand as ossuaries holding the remains of a former religious glory. Yesterday's glory is today's tourist destination. Whitewashed tombs may appear gentle on the eye, but they are full of the rotting bones of white theologies, where the stench of all manner of unclean Eurocentric religious theological propositions designed to exclude the spiritual contributions of the world's colonized offend the nostrils, choking and suffocating those seeking life. These sacred crypts reek with the decay of Eurocentric Christianity, captured by demagogues, and bring forth a foul odor of faith laced with fear and hatred, hoping to procure and secure votes from those whose ears are tickled by patriotic rhetoric. It is worth repeating: such a Christianity—the Christianity of so many Euro-Americans—is dying. Let the dead bury their dead!

Who Is Killing Christianity?

The gospel is slowly dying in the hands of so-called Christians, with evangelicals supplying the morphine drip. Christ's message of love, peace, and liberation, has been distorted and disfigured by Trumpish flimflammers who made a Faustian bargain for the sake of expediency, whose licentious desire for ultraconservative Supreme Court justices trumped God's call to judge justly. These Euro-American Christians have made a preferential option for the golden calf over and against the Golden Rule as they revel in an unadulterated power grab, deeming white privilege to be more attractive than waiting for the inheritance promised to the meek. White Christianity has more than a simple PR problem; it is inherently problematic.

When I write *white Christianity*, you might think that I am generalizing and essentializing a broad Euro-American demographic group based solely on the pigment of their skin. However, ontological whiteness has *nothing* to do with skin pigmentation. This is important, so I will say it again: the word *white* in my usage has nothing to do with the color of one's skin. Instead, it has to do with worldview, a way of being, thinking, and reasoning morally. A *white Christian* can be black, Latinx, Muslim, or atheist. While it might be easier for those with whiter skin to embrace white Christianity, those of us who would never be considered white by our physical appearance have also had our minds so colonized that it is

4

difficult to break free from this white, Christian milieu. Even when the periphery rebels, it can do so only in conversation with and in relationship to the white, Christian center, as illustrated by this very book. We seek prophets who can raise our consciousness to distinguish the difference between a form of Christianity that has been legitimized and normalized through time in the fiber of the life and culture of the United States and a Christianity based on the words and action of a certain brown, Jewish, Middle Easterner called Yeshua.

One can only cringe when witnessing self-proclaimed religious leaders swap their prophetic voice for the satisfying porridge at the emperor's banquet table. The votes were counted: 58 percent of Protestants voted for Trump in 2016; 60 percent of white Catholics voted for Trump; 61 percent of Mormons voted for Trump; 81 percent of white evangelicals voted for Trump![5] These individuals—Protestants, Catholics, Mormons, and evangelicals—share more than an ethnic identity. They share a cultural identity: white Christian. They voted for a person who promised them power and standing even though his entire life repudiates everything Christ modeled and taught. Those who confess to regularly attending church are among his greatest supporters. False prophets have arisen in the land representing the empty husk of white Christianity as exemplified by Jerry Falwell Jr.'s hustle for Donald Trump, an owner of strip clubs and an unrepentant bedswerver. Infidelity within serial marriage becomes the newest benchmark of virtue as Falwell publicly compares

Trump to Jesus Christ. But as troubling as it may be to equate vulgar politicians to Jesus, the Christology they profess tells us more about the political culture from which their Jesus narrative arises than about who Jesus was historically or theologically. These Jesus-creators, in their cosmic fight against whomever they have designated to be the enemies of Christ, implement oppressive structures that politically protect their accumulated privileges. The Jesus whom they create in their own image is, not surprisingly, all too often homophobic, xenophobic, and misanthropic. Such a Jesus celebrates wealth. Such a Jesus builds walls. Such a Jesus separates children from their parents. Such a Jesus fears Muslims. Such a Jesus votes for Donald Trump. MAGA ("Make America Great Again") disguises itself as WWJD ("What Would Jesus Do?").

Trump brags about having nothing to ask God to forgive, contradicting the foundational Christian doctrine that everyone falls short of the glory of God. Nonetheless, the guardians of Eurocentric morality, like James Dobson, attempt to convince us that Trump is a "baby Christian." And while I might agree with the "baby" depiction, I cannot help but doubt the "Christian" part. Like the rich young ruler who was unwilling to use his wealth to alleviate the poverty of the masses, the justifiers of the affluent endanger their claims to the eschatological promises of God when they safeguard and spiritually defend their power and privileges rather than demand justice for the least of these. No one obtains occupancy in heaven without a reference letter from the world's dispossessed. God's reign does not belong to the racist, to the sexist, to the homophobic, to the classist, nor to the xenophobic, despite what public profession of faith they may or may not have made. The promises of God are neither for the oppressor nor for those complicit in oppression, regardless of how "churchy" they may be or which commandments they selectively keep. Believing in Jesus is never sufficient, for even the demons believe and tremble at his name. When Jesus encounters the rich young rulers, then and now, he rejects what they claim to believe for what they actually do as a response to the hungry, the thirsty, the naked, the alien in our midst, the infirm, and the incarcerated.

The Gospels of Jesus Christ are politically charged, revolutionary documents. Yet many Euro-American religious leaders in megachurches and well-paid theologians in comfortable ivory towers exert great energy to neuter and domesticate the political call for justice that resonates in the words of Jesus. The radicalness of the Gospels—a message usually missed by the privileged living in nice houses within the heart of the empire—is watered down. The Jesus narratives, at their core, are anticolonial literature about a native resident displaced by the invading imperial power. The Gospel narratives depict a careful dance between Rome, the colonizer, and Jesus, the colonized. Not far from the story-telling surface is the real-world dynamic of experiencing the consequences of empire. We see it throughout Jesus's everyday life and how he responded to the circumstances brought about by the economic and political occupation of Judea. He answered questions concerning paying tribute to Caesar, constantly faced danger for preaching about another reign or kingdom more powerful than the one to which Jews were subjugated, and finally was charged with being a rival sovereign ("king of the Jews") and sentenced to death. The very audience who first heard the words of Jesus were his colonized compatriots, many of whom held an abiding hatred toward the Roman oppressors. From this colonized space, then and now, the gospel message is shaped and formed. Ignoring this reality leads to false remembrance, if not pure delusion.

This realization of the gospel's political edge was expressed by Pope Francis as he boarded his plane leaving Mexico for Rome in 2016. He urged the modern-day empire of the United States to address the "humanitarian crisis" on its southern border. This is what religious leaders—regardless of their faith tradition—are called to do; they are meant to urge all of us to be more humane toward our fellow global sojourners. Not surprisingly, then-candidate Trump was appalled that his faith was challenged. Calling the pope's comments "disgraceful," Trump goes on to say, "No leader, especially a religious leader, should have the right to question another man's religion or faith."[6] Because white, evangelical Christianity reduces faith to the individual who depends on a personal relationship with Christ, the communal aspects and responsibilities of the gospel can be disregarded and discarded. Even more bizarre, Jerry Falwell Jr. defends Trump by claiming, "Jesus never intended to give instructions to political leaders on how to run a country."[7] Let the sweet irony of his pronouncement sink in for a moment. After all, it was his father, Jerry Falwell Sr., who galvanized the Christian Right as a political religious movement by crusading against civil rights. Specifically, Falwell Sr. railed against *Brown v. Board of Education*. He denounced Martin Luther King Jr. as a communist subversive. Private Christian schools became the answer for circumventing integration, protecting little, white Sally from sitting next to a black boy.

So who then is the Christian? Is it Trump? Is it Falwell? Is it another spokesperson for Eurocentric nationalist Christianity? Is it the pope? Is it the author of this book? If a tree is known by its fruit, then the answer should be easy to determine. Jesus gives us a vision of a day when the heavens will roll away and the son of humanity returns in all his glory, accompanied by the host of heaven, gathering all the people and separating them as a shepherd divides the sheep from the goats. He will invite the sheep to enter the reign prepared for them since the foundation of the earth. "For I was hungry and rather than vote to eliminate the Supplemental Nutrition Assistance Program, you gave me some food to eat. I was thirsty, and rather than condemn me to drink out of Flint's lead-tainted faucets, you provided me with clean and safe drinking water. I was naked, and rather than criminalize my appearance by passing antivagrancy laws, you clothed me. I was an alien, without proper documentation, and rather than debate whether to build walls—visible or invisible—to separate my brownness from your vanilla suburbs, you welcomed me. I was infirm, wasting away, and rather than attempt to repeal Obamacare, you worked to create a sustainable medical system that could heal me. I was incarcerated, and rather than privatize the prison system, which profits by maintaining high brown and black occupancy, you sought to develop a just judicial system not dependent on profiting off the existence of my dark body."

When the virtuous, as well as the condemned, ask how their salvation, or lack thereof, was determined, Jesus replies that he himself was the person avoided, ignored, or shunned. Jesus does more than simply show empathy for the poor and oppressed. He does more than simply express some paternalistic concern. Jesus *is* the poor and oppressed. "Inasmuch as you did it to one of these, the least of my people, you did it to me" (Matt. 25:40).[8] If you want to gaze into the eyes of Jesus, look into the eyes of the undocumented immigrant caught and abused while crossing artificial borders. If you want to place your hand in the hand of the one who calmed the waters, then shake the hand of the homeless person. The sheep are not separated from the goats by the criteria of which faith tradition they claim, or which house of worship they attend, or which doctrines they profess, or even whether they have made a confession of faith. Sheep and goats are separated by what they did or did not do to the least of these. And truly I say unto you—because of their faithful care for their communities—Muslims, atheists, Buddhists, and Wiccans are entering the kingdom of God ahead of Euro-American Christians.

Christianity in the United States sleepwalks toward apostasy. If the purpose of religious and theological critical thought concerning the personhood of Jesus is to serve humanity by transforming the normative oppressive social structures into the justice-based reality preached by Jesus, then neither Donald Trump nor any other presidential candidate (either Republican or Democratic) comes close. For Euro-American Christians to seek saviors among politicians is to find anti-Christs. To honor the gospel message of liberation, Christians must hold politicians accountable to the demands of justice, not crown them as God's chosen. If this is true, then we must ask whether those who use, misuse, and abuse the disenfranchised—even if they are running for president—are actually Christians. And more importantly, are those who pledge allegiance to oppressors—even though they call themselves born-again evangelical Christians—saved? Only those who refuse to see would claim that Trump is a Christian. His hubristic claims of being without sin are supported by the use of theocratic mirages to distract and deflect truths. We are told Trump is a Christian because those who claim to speak for God—James Dobson, Jerry Falwell Jr., Tony Perkins, Franklin Graham, and Pat Robertson—say he is. But if these self-appointed mouthpieces for God actually do speak for the divine, then God surely is a simpleton. Where are the erudite sages of yesteryear who struggled with complex theological questions? Can God no longer speak through an Augustine, an Aquinas, or a Teresa of Avila? Are our modern self-proclaimed spokespersons for the divine an indication of God's shrinking bailiwick? The unsophisticated pronouncements of these ultracrepidarian spokespersons for Euro-American Christianity condemn God to the realm of hackneyed, pollyannish platitudes.

White churchgoers have historically been, and continue to be, the greatest existential hazard for humanity, especially for the dispossessed and disinherited. Since the foundation of the republic, white Christians have reigned supreme in North America by using invasion, genocide, and slavery as instruments of political control. During the 1980s, evangelicals positioned themselves as the moral voice of the nation. This is a constituency who gained a foothold in the political process by helping—contrary to their rhetoric—a divorced actor (deeply interested in astrology!) win the presidency over and against a Baptist Sunday School teacher. Falwell and Graham's fathers lived during a time when they had a say in political discourse. Those were no doubt evangelicalism's political golden years, in which personal piety buttressed conservative social positions.

And yet, after years of unchecked hegemony, many white Christians now feel less secure. It has become more difficult to exist in a world being pulled toward inclusion when one has become accustomed, for centuries, to an exalted and exclusive place in society. The birthright of white privilege is being undermined as the previously voiceless are effectively demanding a more pluralistic social configuration. The call to "Make America Great Again" is a demand to return to an era where my brown skin would have relegated me to mopping the floors at my graduate school rather than teaching in its classrooms. The once-powerful religious Right had tremendous sway and power within the GOP (God's Own Party!) and the nation, and it is natural for those losing their footing to want to reclaim some of their standing. But at what price? When we remember that the message of the biblical prophets usually revolved around the theme of economic justice, or that Jesus spoke more about money than any other topic, we are left dumbfounded by the failure of Christian churches (evangelical and mainline), who claim to be Bible-believing disciples within prosperous nations, to broach one of the main themes (if not the main theme) of the biblical text: justice.

Our quest is for a Jesus not captured by the dominant Eurocentric culture. The white Jesus is damning to the disenfranchised. The world's dispossessed search for a Jesus who resonates specifically with those excluded by the hegemonic Eurocentric Christianity. The Jesus of the United States of America to whom Donald Trump and his apologists bend their knees can never save the disenfranchised who are consigned to the underside of whiteness. The crucial first step toward saying yes to God, yes to salvation, yes to liberation, and yes to our communities is to say no to oppression masked by a nationalist Christianity draped in the Stars and Stripes.

Embracing Hypocrisy

Values and virtues seem to matter only when they can be hurled at opposing candidates. Protectors of family values who once feigned righteous indignation over "scandalous" photos of Michelle Obama's armpits offer multiple mulligans to a Manhattan sybarite with a history of misogynist comments and payoffs to a porn star and Playboy model in exchange for discretion. Or as Tony Perkins of the Family Research Council infamously quipped concerning infidelities: Trump gets a "do-over."[9] The same Franklin Graham who held Bill Clinton accountable in 1998 for his sexual misdeeds, claiming that his private conduct had public consequences, claims in 2018 that Trump's sex life is "nobody's business."[10] When Robert Jeffress, pastor of First Baptist Church in Dallas, dismisses the president's sexcapades with a porn star stating, "Even if it's true, it doesn't matter;"[11] he is preaching that God's commandments do not matter, that Christian morality does not matter, that family values do not matter. Surely we can all remember Jesus's enduring words, "You have heard that it was said 'Do not commit adultery.' *But I say to you that whosoever does may pay discreetly and get a do-over*" (Trumpian adaptation of Matt. 5:49). Biblical teachings can always be disregarded when one worships the partisan God. Jeffress is quick to blame 9/11 on America's sinfulness while shamelessly sporting a log in his eye. Every immoral, illicit, irreverent, and illegal act by Christian nationalism is seemingly permissible as long as it serves a higher political purpose. The ends justify the means. All is overlooked for the price of an embassy in Jerusalem.

One might have hoped that evangelical leaders would live into their ministerial roles when they planned a sit-down meeting with the president in June 2018 to discuss the swirling sex scandals. Instead, the meeting was designed to rally and reassure conservative voters. Ralph Reed of the Faith and Freedom Coalition claimed it was "highly dubious" that Trump's trysts would substantially erode support for the president or negatively impact turnout during the 2018 midterm elections, but the meeting's organizers were taking no chances. One of the goals of the gathering was to frame voting during the midterm elections as a civic duty of Christians.[12] Evangelical guardians of morality within the United States have sold Jesus for more than thirty pieces of silver. They have made a more lucrative bargain. Since they get to be in the Oval Office where crucial political decisions happen, they can ensure their multimillion dollar empires will remain safeguarded from governmental scrutiny. The payoff for acquiescence to the seduction of the church by the state leads to increases in their tax-exempt proceeds garnered by fleecing the widow of her mite. Profits over prophets!

The nationalist Christianity of which I speak—the Christianity of the Perkinses, the Falwells, the Grahams, and all the other male spiritual icons and political hacks—has nothing to do with faith, and even less to do with Jesus. Divine providence has absolutely nothing to do with the election of Trump. Euro-Americans hustled a white nationalism that worships the God of empire, the God of wealth, and the God of militarism by supporting isolationism and anti-Federalism. They bow their knees before Moloch and sacrifice their children to the God of the National Rifle Association to secure the salvation of their precious religious fetish, the gun. White Christianity has nothing to do with the Judeo-Christian God of the biblical text. Nationalist Christianity is but another political movement with a very thin Christian veneer used to manipulate spirituality and maintain white dominance and Eurocentric privileges. Eurocentric Christianity is truly an opiate that numbs the disenfranchised with promises of the hereafter in order to distract them from suffering imposed in the here-and-now. Social justice ceases to be for the now, relegated instead to some ethereal future where every wrong will be righted and every tear wiped away. This opiate keeps those who use it on a consistent high that ignores complicity in social structures designed to be death-dealing to the dispossessed.

But Trump is not an aberration. He is indeed the wished-for creation of white Christians. When these Christians identify Trump with Christianity, one is left to wonder about the true nature of Christianity. Trump is neither the first, nor will he be the last, white supremacist elected president of the United States by adherents of a nationalist Christianity. In the past, the United States elected slavers (e.g., George Washington), rapists of women of color (e.g., Thomas Jefferson), Indian-killers (e.g., Andrew Jackson), and avowed supporters of the Ku Klux Klan (e.g., Woodrow Wilson). The election of Trump—a bon viveur, adulterer, liar, racist, and sexual predator—by a so-called Christian nation is not an aberration; it is the norm. Rather than being the salt of the earth, white Christians serve as a shield against those who question the immorality of the president of the United States.

Trump has become a modern-day King Cyrus, the Persian King in 539 BCE used by God for God's purposes. Like Cyrus, the American president need not be perfect to be used by God to advance the special interests of Euro-Americans. The gospel is pimped for the cheap coins of partisan politics when white Christians lay hands upon the incarnation of every vice Jesus condemned in order to advance their political agenda. Yet nothing resembling the teachings of Jesus has emerged from this administration. Those who consider Trump to be a modern-day Cyrus are, in reality, worshipping a frail and feeble God and providing spiritual backing to today's Caesar so they can dream of tomorrow's theocracy. Eurocentric Christians approach supremacist politicians with open arms and legs, wrapping the cross in the flag, as Mike Pence, vice president of the United States, continuously does, introducing himself as "a Christian, a conservative, and a Republican"[13]—as if the terms are synonymous and interchangeable.

White Christianity in the United States has ceased being a religious faith tradition rooted in the teachings of Christ. It is not focused on justice and the betterment of humanity. Rather, it has made a pact with the devil for the sake of Supreme Court appointments. While justifying their choice with pro-life rhetoric, they bloody their hands through their allegiance to death-dealing policies that disproportionately impact the poor, the undocumented, and the queer. Pro-life Christians in the United States who today want to build walls to drive brown bodies into the desert to die are the ideological descendants of pro-life pilgrims and slave masters whose invasion, genocide, enslavement, and rape epitomize the legacy of white Christianity. During those years of expansion, slavery, Jane and Jim Crow, and Manifest Destiny, any who dared speak a word of truth to power faced expulsion, if not death. Survival—financial and physical—depended on self-discipline, tailoring the gospel so as not to conflict with human-rights atrocities.

The rituals and practices of white Christianity within the United States developed over centuries to create an empire on the backs of those who fell short of the white, male ideal. Today their spiritual descendants injudiciously rush to present a non-Christian as God's faithful servant—chosen by God *himself* —even if it means continuously pimping the body of Christ to the highest political bidder. No political party, neither Republicans nor Democrats, is ordained by God. No president, emperor, or prime minister is a present-day Messiah.

And yet, like some Borgia or Medici pope, a corrupt clergy crowns and defends their new emperor. As long as this Christianity founded and sustained on white supremacy continues to reign supreme, Euro-American Christians will continue to flock to antichrists.

So why should we be surprised that a nationalist Christianity has nothing to do with belief or faith in the personhood and teachings of Jesus Christ? After all, it never did. Obviously, Christianity did not die because of Donald Trump's election. Any Christianity that could so readily ally itself with such a candidate and such policies was already gravely ill. What Trump's election made impossible is to continue pretending that white Christianity had any shred of a moral foundation. After 2016, white Christians lost any and all moral authority they might have possessed to say anything concerning the probity of anyone. The mask has slipped to reveal the undergirding racism—in all of its vile glory—that always existed beneath the façade of holy and pure superiority. In a nation divided between those who view themselves as exceptional and those who recognize the racism of such a position, neutrality and silence in the face of injustice make those muted complicit with said racism— whether they like it or not. Clinging to Christianity as the solution to what ails our nation is insufficient because white Christianity has crucified the faith of the oppressed on its crosses of racism, classism, sexism, heterosexism, and all the other -isms imaginable.

But I'm So Exceptional

The United States, since its foundation, has suffered from schizophrenia (from two Greek words that mean "split mind"). With one mind, Americans claim radical inclusion "with liberty and justice for all," while with the other mind they reinforce social structures of exclusion to benefit the few through the loss of liberty and justice for the many. Eurocentric Christianity—a manipulative, racist ideology that has nothing to do with faith, or spirituality, or even Christ—is a colonial, conquering political philosophy that for centuries has worn a religious veneer to justify thievery, enslavement, and genocide for the betterment of whites. To "Make America Great Again" recharges and reenergizes white supremacy by reclaiming and restoring a threatened birthright. The promise of "an American dream," regardless of race or creed, conflicts with the dominant perspective of a white chosen people who are sole beneficiaries of God's grace and promises, evident in the removal of the phrase "a nation of immigrants" from the website and mission statement of the US Citizenship and Immigration Services in early 2018. The mythology of exceptionalism justifies atrocities that would be condemned if perpetrated by any other nation. Since the establishment of the CIA, the United States has continually influenced the elections of other countries (and has sometimes overthrown democracies outright, as in Iran, Guatemala, and Chile), but when Russia influences our own election, it becomes wrong.

Why is it right for us and wrong for them? Because we are exceptional. Exceptionality jingoism suspends the United States' ethical and moral imperatives while reinforcing a national arrogance that prevents constructive dialogue aimed at forming a more just and liberating global order.

This exceptionalism, which treats whites as the new Israel and the United States as the New Jerusalem, "a shining city upon a hill," was launched over a century before the founding of the republic. It was first voiced by Puritan John Winthrop in a 1630 sermon while he was en route to the so-called new world, which the colonists planned to invade and conquer in Christ's name. This religious, romantic portrayal of the Eurocentric mission in terms of light illuminating the path for the rest of humanity created the American exceptionalism that permeated the worldview and speeches of both moderate Democrats like John F. Kennedy and conservative Republicans like Ronald Reagan.

God, then, becomes the author of a US exceptionalism justifying *his* white, chosen people while relegating all nonwhites to the margins of society by normalizing, spiritualizing, and legitimizing atrocities committed against Indians, blacks, Latinxs, Asians, Jews, Muslims—in short, all nonwhites and non-Christians. Whites belong; nonwhites are merely guests. The greatness of the United States was possible only because of the perceived divine right of Pilgrims to steal from the indigenous people their stored winter provisions, all the while offering God thanksgiving for *his* merciful bounty.

America could never have become great if not for God-fearing Pilgrims stealing Indian lands. America could never have become great if not for the genocide of these Indians by those who followed the Pilgrims, believing it was God's will to purify the promised land of its modern-day Canaanites. And while some nations, like Turkey, ignore the genocide of the Armenians; and others, like Germany, attempt to repent from their genocide of the Jews, the United States, led by Trump, unapologetically celebrates an exceptionalism which justified the genocide of indigenous people, bragging that "our ancestors . . . tamed a continent" and "we are not going to apologize for America."[14]

America could never have become great without stealing black bodies and their labor for profit, north and south of the Mason-Dixon Line. America could never have become great without stealing the sovereignty of all peoples who stood in the path of Manifest Destiny, a religious mandate to invade nations throughout the Américas and steal land, resources, and cheap labor from those requiring civilization and Christianization. Today's exceptionalism is the latest manifestation of a white, Christian supremacy that insures the vast majority of the world's resources flow to support 6 percent of the global population. America could never have become great unless it had embraced a new age of blatant and brazen missionary zeal for white supremacy. Only white immigrants need apply, for Trump prefers migration from countries like Norway, which is 83 percent ethnically white, as opposed to the "shithole" countries of Haiti, El Salvador, and all of Africa.[15] One could probably add to the list of shithole countries Jesus's birthplace, Galilee, from where nothing good comes.

American exceptionalism is the stuff of empires that historically claim that normative global ethical rules and democratic virtues do not apply to them. The dominant culture's Christianity that reinforces Americans as the new chosen people is disproportionately responsible for much of the terror experienced by nonwhites globally, an acceptable terrorism because it is masked by an American exceptionalism ordained by divine right. But on that last day, those for whom America was made great will cry out "Lord, Lord did we not do great things in your name?" only to hear in reply, "Away from me you wicked and evil people for I never knew you. For you preached against murder while killing, preached against adultery while raping."

If the essence of the gospel message is that it gives life, and life abundantly (John 10:10), then everything that brings death, and death profusely, even if it is presented as Christian, cannot be of God. My colleague James Cone called this white Christianity satanic, but I believe it is worse than something simply evil. Eurocentric Christianity is a political ideology responsible for more enslavement, more death, and more misery than any other worldview throughout recorded history. Christianity in the United States may have its roots in Europe, specifically the crusades, the Inquisition, the religious wars, and the rise of empires, but the United States' manifestation of Christianity lifted human depravity to all new unholy levels. The white Jesus—iconized by Warner Sallman—is indeed satanic, and those who hustle this demon are, as Paul reminds us, "false apostles, deceitful workers, masquerading as apostles of Christ. And no wonder, for Satan himself masquerades as an angel of light. It is not surprising, then, if his servants also masquerade as servants of righteousness. Their end will be what their actions deserve" (2 Cor. 11:13–15).

Haters Gonna Hate

To reject Eurocentric Christianity is often to be labeled a heretic, to be labeled an angry person, or to be labeled a hater. As a minister of the gospel of Jesus Christ, I have been called to proclaim good news and shine a light on everything that brings forth death. White Christianity in the United States damns Jesus. An underlying problem with a white Christianity is its relegation of Christian belief to the personal, to the private. Simply believe, and you shall be saved! This was, after all, Billy Graham's message. Graham did integrate his revivals in the 1950s. Yet he opposed the Civil Rights Acts and criticized Martin Luther King Jr. for attempting to bring about a different reality by changing laws rather than changing hearts. With his eyes on the eschatological promise, Graham railed against any social program (such as the New Deal, the Fair Deal, the New Frontier, and the Great Society) designed to alleviate human suffering. Fiercely pro-capitalist and anti-socialist, Graham—although an extremely pious man—believed social ills could only be salved until Jesus's second coming. While Martin Luther King Jr. dreamed "that one day little black boys and girls will be holding hands with little white boys and girls," Graham remarked that the dream must be deferred: "Only when Christ comes again will the little children of Alabama walk hand in hand with little black children."[16] Meanwhile, he remained paranoid over some future world government stripping United States Christians of their rights, thus calling for believers to elect officials who shared his delusions, which they did by electing traffickers of the Christian faith.

For evangelical Christians like the Grahams, one can continue engaging in everything Jesus preached against as long as one decides to give oneself over to Jesus in some theoretical or partial sense that does not necessarily entail following or even intending to follow his own teachings and example. "Cheap grace"—as Adam Clayton Powell Sr. preached—has given us a faith tradition that demands nothing of us. For some, it is as simple as reciting some incantation like a "Sinner's Prayer." Many Christians in the United States actually see concepts of social justice as antithetical to the gospel! White Christian fundamentalists and social commentators (such as Glenn Beck) warn their listeners to flee congregations that promote social justice. They proclaim acceptance of Jesus but deny Jesus's message by preaching against social justice as if it were a sin. For Christianity in the United States, moral endeavor becomes a matter of speculating about what is ethical rather than rolling up our sleeves and bending the arc of the moral universe toward justice.

While our current nationalist Christianity is the overall legitimatized norm, it is nonetheless presented as a private matter. As long as Jesus remains a merely personal savior, Christianity can be tamed, demanding no action to implement Jesus's public teachings on how to live justly. Scholars like historian Martin Marty have argued that the United States is a secular society that has secured religious institutions in a boxed-in space, relegating Christianity to the private sphere while excluding it from public life. Christianity in the United States, as a civil religion, serves to make society an idol. In this way, it is possible to ignore the crimes against humanity upon which the United States was established by hypocritically pivoting the religious discourse to personal piety.

Unrepentant Indian-killers and former slaveholders are still considered Christians by many because they accepted Jesus as their personal savior and thus now reside in heaven. For example, James P. Boyce and John A. Broadus, avowed racists and chaplains in the Confederate army, played key roles in founding my alma mater, the Southern Baptist Theological Seminary. They will not be found among the cloud of witnesses. Make no mistake, there are no oppressors in the presence of God. It would be easier for a camel to go through the eye of a needle than for an oppressor to walk upon the streets of gold.

God and country becomes one and the same, where being a good Christian means being a good "American" and vice versa. This patriotic Christianity reflected the conquering spirit of those who invaded this hemisphere, constructing an exclusive interpretation that fused and confused white supremacy with salvation. Salvation is limited to those whom the social structures are designed to privilege, and those of their "inferiors" (as they suppose) who embrace assimilation with colonized minds. "God is on our side" becomes the nationalist Christian battle cry as we march like Christian soldiers unto war. Those not saved stand as enemies of God and *his* chosen, sanctioning Euro-American Christians to become the instrument to purify the faith and the land. Divine permission is given to offer either the cross or the sword. This corruption of Christianity requires the transformation of the prince of peace to the wager of war. Yeshua, the messenger of love, becomes Mars, the god of war.

To save Jesus from those claiming to be his heirs, we must wrench him from the hands of white Christians who forged a nationalist Christianity constipated with hate and fear—fear of Muslims, fear of the undocumented, fear of blacks, and fear of everything queer. Hate, of course, is a strong word, implying severe loathing to the point of desiring or instigating extreme harm to the object hated. Hatred is neither an emotion nor a sentiment, but willful praxis. One hates because one acts in a hateful manner. There is no better word than hatred to describe the current administration's actions toward those falling outside of the protective sphere of white Christianity. Hatred simply won. Thanks to the 2016 election, we have progressed from a political correctness that masked racism and ethnic discrimination to a full-blown demonstration of revenge for the years in which people of color strived to hold this country accountable for rhetorical concepts like equality, justice, and respect for diversity.

White Christians may insist that racism was not a primary motivation for casting their votes for Trump and that their votes came from "forgotten Americans" who were economically struggling. But I reject such analysis. The causes are not a simple matter of either-or. They felt forgotten because they believed "those damned aliens" were taking their jobs and, thanks to affirmative action, undeserving welfare queens and young bucks were draining the system. Every vote cast for the Dreamers' nightmare, every vote cast for the proctor of religious tests to exclude Muslims, every vote cast for one to whom black lives never mattered was a vote for racism using economics as an excuse. And the true nature of that vote became obvious within twenty-four hours of the election. Mark Potok of the Southern Poverty Law Center, an organization that tracks hate crimes, documented a rash of hate rhetoric and racist graffiti on campuses around the country. Should we be surprised that hate crimes, in 2017, rose by 12.5 percent in the largest US cities, the highest total in over a decade?[17] What is truly telling is the deafening silence from the president, who conspicuously fails to repudiate these incidents and chastise perpetrators of violence in his name.

What all these white perpetrators of hatred have in common is an anti-intellectual paranoia, labeling thinkers as elitists, while embracing falsehoods and conspiracies. Rather than standing up as responsible politicians, journalists, and religious leaders to counsel and dissuade those choosing death—specifically the death of the Others—many "leaders" instead conform to the crassest stereotypes, inciting fear in exchange for support, popularity, or increased personal revenue. Yes, we can dismiss those perpetrating hate crimes as deranged ignoramuses, but the fingerprints of the president and the so-called Christian church that praises the God of Trump, along with all those responsible for stoking fear to garner votes, are also all over these incidents. Politicians have usually employed the raw emotions of fear and hatred, powerful manipulative tools that provide a lazy electorate with simplistic answers to their economic distress. Americans suffer from a recurring amnesia when it comes to their historic complicity with racism and ethnic discrimination. Always under the surface, fear and hatred stand ready to reemerge, as we are currently witnessing.

The majority of white Christians voted for Trump. They demonstrated an abhorrence to what they perceive as a nightmarish vision of the United States rooted in the concerns of families of color and queer families, who demand dignity and respect. Every hate crime committed reveals their complicity with centuries of whites spiritually justifying hatred. This nationalist Christianity is responsible for every person of color whose vote was suppressed, every Latinx child left orphaned because of parents deported, every woman who lives in fear of sexual predators, every queer person denied the basic human right of whom to love. The hateful policies emanating from the current administration are reflected in the hatred for people of color demonstrated when Trump redlined to prevent tenants of color from living in his buildings, stoked the fearmongering that sent the innocent Central Park Five to prison, and, as president, defended white nationalists in Charlottesville. This hatred reflects the will of the American people and the Christianity that they profess.

Only hatred would advocate an immigration policy that separates children from their mothers. But why should we be surprised at a nation whose history is based on separating children from mothers, whether they be black children shipped to other plantations or indigenous children shipped to Indian schools? Nothing has changed. Christians may shed indignant crocodile tears for these children of the past, but their stony and callous hearts refuse to break for today's Latinx children facing similar separations. What is it about the white supremacy of both conservatives and liberals that condones such barbarism? What kind of religion tolerates separating crying children from nursing mothers?

We recognized this hatred when a president and a willing nation turned a blind eye to some 3.4 million United States citizens on the island of Puerto Rico, where about half of the population still lacked power three months after being devastated by Hurricane María. And while Trump lobbed paper towels at desperate people, taking comfort that "only" sixty-four died because of the storm, brown bodies continue to be historically miscounted and misrepresented within the consciousness and imagination of the United States, since the actual death count was over forty-six hundred, according to *The New England Journal of Medicine*.[18] But why should whites care about an island full of Latinxs? Imagine if the states of Maine, New Hampshire, and Vermont, which combined have an equal number of residents as Puerto Rico, faced such a humanitarian crisis. I am sure the full force of the federal government would move heaven and earth to restore power and protect life there because, after all, these three New England states are predominately (96 percent) white. Trump's wrath toward brown bodies was, from the start, a major focus of his run for the presidency. Kicking off his campaign with explicit unadulterated hatred, Trump energized his deplorable racist base by depicting Latinxs as drug-runners, criminals, and rapists. Throughout the campaign, chants of "build the wall" from Trump supporters exposed a deep loathing for Latinxs.

White Christians also cheered as Trump made Islamic xenophobia central to his presidential quest, fulfilling his promise to ban Muslims from entering the country and thereby creating chaos and untold misery at our international airports. Whites may fear Muslims, but communities of color fear armed whites more. Most of those who commit mass shootings within the United States are not Muslims but whites (many of whom are racists portrayed as "lone wolves"), whose views are encouraged by politicians, protected by gun lobbyists, and celebrated by antigovernment Christian fanatics. Charles Kurzman's 2017 study documented how law enforcement agencies throughout the nation agree that threats from Muslim extremists are minuscule compared to the threat from right-wing extremists.[19]

Throughout his presidency, chants of "Trump! Trump! Trump!" (in Trinitarian form) continue to be used to marginalize nonwhites. Many perceive the chant as a racial jeer that encourages and empowers white Christian xenophobia. What other name of a president has become a racist taunt to strike alarm and anxiety among nonwhites? And the very fact that the word "Trump" is used in this manner demonstrates the depth of the hatred expressed by those invoking his name and of the one who carries the name. Is it surprising that a March 2018 study published in the journal *Epidemiology* documented an increase in violence in cities that hosted Trump rallies? Christopher Morrison's study demonstrated that an average of 2.3 more assaults were reported on the days of Trump's rallies. No corresponding link between assaults and rallies was detected in the gatherings of his Democratic rival, Hillary Clinton. Trump's calling on supporters to rough up hecklers during his rallies, even though he said he was just joking or offering to pay the legal fees for perpetrators of violence confirms Morrison's assertion that the association of violence with Trump is "a phenomenon that's unique to Donald Trump."[20] One cannot simultaneously shout the name of Jesus, which represents love, and the name of Trump, which represents hate. Like the fool who tries to serve two masters, they will hate one and love the other. Any faith that loves hate may exert great power, but that faith at its core remains spiritually dead.

Stupid Is as Stupid Does

When repressive structures must be sustained, truth is always the first casualty. Truth must be crucified, ignorance and prejudices must be mobilized, and Christianity must be nullified if the hope is to "Make America Great Again." Nationalist Christianity can maintain its privileged space within the new society Trump is creating only by promulgating his bunkum and promoting his ignorance. Academics may very well share some responsibility for a world where reality and truth are whatever one claims they are. What were the unintended consequences of embracing postmodernity in its attempt to deconstruct philosophical and religious truth, where truth was reduced to a product of a power suspicious of all metanarratives? In dismissing all absolutes by equalizing all perspectives, have we validated the current administration's war on empiricism where factual truths are dismissed as constructs of liberal coastal elites in the media, the academy, and the scientific community? Actual events become fake news. Lies become alternative facts. Scientific records demonstrating global warming are dismissed as a hoax. Ronald Reagan's Freudian slip probably says it best: "Facts are stupid things." The Jesus who called for our yays to be yay and our nays to be nay (see Matt. 5:37) is dismissed by Euro-American Christians who favor political positioning over and against truth. Truth seems important only when it serves the purpose of advancing the nationalist Christian agenda.

The truth of nationalistic Christianity is undergirded by a lie that must be so extreme and exaggerated that simple minds can be easily seduced. Even the educated, who should know better, suspend disbelief because the lie advances their political agendas. The importance of the lie rests in its ability to delegitimize, to destabilize, and to demoralize legal authorities. An entire political career can be built on a lie such as "the president was born in Kenya." Regardless of birth certificates, the lie fuels racist fears of having a black man occupying the White House. The lie keeps the embers of hatred simmering while keeping the snollygoster in the spotlight, masquerading as a crusader for truth. When the initiator of the birther movement tweeted a new lie, his purpose was to undermine the democratic process and explain away his loss of the popular election by almost 2.9 million votes. Claiming the only reason he fell short was because of the three million "illegals" who voted in California, he reinforced the fear and hatred for Latinxs by accusing the excluded of undermining democracy. No evidence is necessary; no verification need be provided. The burden of proof lies not with the accuser, but with the accused. In the era of Trump, something is true even when proven false.

Christianity in the United States accepts and adopts the lie while anointing the falsifier because the lie serves a crucial function: it maintains focus on imaginary threats to white America. "Put America First" has always and continues to mean "Put Whites First." But why should we pretend to be shocked or surprised? After all, we are speaking of a political prevaricator who changed his views on abortion, who switched political parties in 2011, who supported gender-neutral bathrooms at Trump Tower only later, as president, to rescind transgender bathroom guidelines—all so he could become and remain president. The moral foundation is whatever the moral foundation needs to be for Trump's Christian base to support him. No lie has yet been uttered that is too odious or outrageous for the faithful. Nationalist Christianity always has been, and continues to be a lie—no matter how much they may engage in gaslighting—because there is no preferential epistemological option for the oppressed.

Mendacities flourish in the new age of ignorance that is embraced by nationalist Christianity, which would rather blame homosexuality for natural disasters than consider the scientific consequences of global warming, such as its contribution to an increase of ever-more-ferocious storms. Such ignorance brings destruction and devastation to God's creation so the few can profit in their continuous rape of Mother Earth. The presidential pivot from politicians' expected exaggerations to bald-faced lies supported by nationalist Christianity is a sign of the times. We stand at the cusp a new age of ignorance reminiscent of the Dark Ages associated with medieval times.

The political lies that Christian leaders call truth for the sake of expedience—or what Trump calls "truthful hyperbole"—fuel the paranoia contributing to the fertile ground where white supremacy and racism thrive. When academia and the educated are demonized, when investigative journalism is dismissed, when the sciences of evolution and climate change are depicted as hoaxes, witlessness is placed on equal footing with rigorous scholarship. "Diversity of thought" becomes the newest euphemism that perverts understanding of fairness by providing those who threaten safety, as witnessed in Charlottesville, public spaces to propagate mistrust and incite violence. This is obvious when we accept at face value the claims of those who deny the Holocaust or the moon landing, in spite of the overwhelming empirical evidence to the contrary. These outrageous views are symptomatic of a society choosing ignorance over enlightenment to selfishly advance its own interest, of an outdated ideology attempting to hold onto supremacy within a society being challenged. Nationalist Christianity that embraces such ignorance is the intellectual progeny of a past age where superstitions backed by the church insisted that the sun revolved around the earth and that illnesses were caused by demons rather than germs.

And yet, with all of our education and access to information via the Internet, nationalist Christianity clings to distrust and ignorance because it prefers the secure, sturdy chains of fear rather than a truth in which we bear responsibility for living as free agents. This situation is exacerbated when Euro-American Christians support politicians who pander for votes by encouraging fear and idiocy in order to get elected. Did not Jesus teach us there is no fear in love because perfect love casts out fear? White Christianity is heretical because it is based on fear and not love. Euro-American Christianity is incapable of love, for it greatly fears nonwhites. Nationalist Christianity emerged as a political response to this white fear. This is a fear demonstrated by invading settlers who always feared Indians would attack to reclaim their stolen land. This is a fear demonstrated by slaveholders who always feared slave revolts by blacks seeking to reclaim their stolen bodies. This is a fear demonstrated by savage capitalists who always feared laborers organizing and striking to reclaim their stolen wages. This is a fear demonstrated by proponents of gunboat diplomacy who always feared migrating Latinxs seeking to reclaim their stolen resources and cheap labor. White Christianity is so fearful it would rather protect its right to bear arms than allow gun control, even as their children perish while sitting in classrooms, sitting in movie theaters, or sitting in houses of worship. The apostasy of white Christianity is rooted in its inability to love those whom they fear and have pushed to their margins.

Perpetuating fear and ignorance helps politicians, who by brownnosing white Christian leaders, get reelected. But here is the real irony. Whites are not the ones under attack. Their fear, unlike that of people of color, is not based on being disenfranchised. Their fear is based on what they might lose, their unearned power, influence, and privileges. Whites represent the majority of those who occupy Wall Street, corporate boardrooms, the White House, Congress, courts, police departments, and elected offices, as well as controlling the largest share of wealth and income in the United States, and thus the world. What the celebration of ignorance produces is the election of truth-manipulators emboldened to protect not only white privilege, but more importantly, class privilege. The unleashing of white supremacy fortified by the celebration of ignorance justifies violent responses because whites are "under attack" or "losing their country," as was demonstrated by the election of a black man to the presidency.

In the matrix of lies masquerading as truth to maintain repression, how is reality discerned? Can an epistemological privilege be given to those most oppressed? Because the marginalized are forced to exist in a society detrimental to their health and wealth, they are forced to master the master's reality for the sake of their very survival, while also knowing what it means to live in their own reality. This "double consciousness" (see W. E. B. Du Bois) provides the dispossessed with a better grasp of reality, of what is true. But rather than privileging the knowledge of the oppressed, Eurocentric Christianity seeks to convert them to whiteness and also to teach them how to fear. We can no longer patiently wait for the dead to bury the dead. Our very survival requires us to dig the graves for this Trumpish Christianity.

2

The Fallacy of Whiteness

Whenever someone I care for, like my wife, attempts to share with me how something I said or did hurt her, I often become defensive. Not wanting to hear how I might have injured her or caused her distress, I become irate. Similarly, when the disenfranchised attempt to enter into a dialogue with those who are privileged, hoping to express deep-seated grievances, the dominant culture can become defensive or even angry. While those in power may be quick to examine or, at times, even acknowledge how the power they hold privileges them, they also use this power to their advantage by directing the discourse, labeling the disenfranchised as angry, not seeing a need to repent, or transforming themselves into the "real" victim.

As a young man in my early twenties, I walked down the aisle and made a public confession, giving my heart to Jesus. The Southern Baptist Evangelical church I joined was a large, loving, predominately white congregation. For the first time, I felt as if I belonged to a group of like-minded people with large hearts. These white folks embraced me as if I were family (or so I thought). These loving, gentle people took it upon themselves to teach me about God, the Bible, and what it meant to be a Christian, as they defined and understood the Word. Among the many lessons they taught were those concerning the sin of homosexuality and the importance of a woman's submission to the man as the God-ordained head of the household. Why would I doubt the very people I admired and wanted to emulate? These were sincere people who extended open arms to me. Surely, they would not purposely lead me astray. They knew their Bibles and were quick to cite chapters and verses, making their subjective interpretation of Holy Writ and understanding of Jesus objective for peoples of all nations. I learned, however, that converting to this form of Christianity meant that I needed to convert, more or less, to the white dominant culture. If I wanted to belong to this group of Christians and make this church my home, I needed the self-discipline to put on whiteface if I desired to remain consistent with my church's conservative worldviews and theology. In effect, I learned to define my faith and myself through the eyes of white supremacy, regardless as to how loving and sincere the oppressors appeared.

Notwithstanding of how genuine and sympathetic white Christians may be, the way they have been taught to read the Bible advocates classism, racism, heterosexism, and misogyny, making them heirs to those who previously used Holy Writ to persecute disenfranchised racial and ethnic groups. Like their spiritual ancestors who perpetrated genocide to "save" heathens and fulfill their Manifest Destiny of occupying stolen land, white Christians continue to commit outrages today, in spite of the sincerity of their faith. Despite the hours they spend on bended knees seeking God's face, they fall into the same mortal sin as their spiritual ancestors in Salem who hung independent-thinking women for witchcraft. Those white Christians from earlier centuries, who used God's Word as a lamp unto their feet and a light unto their path, shamelessly marched forward to enslave Africans, steal Mexicans' land in the southwest, and deny women's basic human rights. From their gilded pedestals erected in white centers of wealth and power, the privileged now gaslight those from whom they benefit into believing that white Christians are the ones being persecuted because of their faith. The God-fearing folks at my church were really nice people who saw themselves under attack for their faith by a secular government and liberal media. Sadly, this type of faith, one truly in denial and blind to its own illness, is an abomination before the Lord.

For a person of color to question the dominant Eurocentric biblical interpretation or to insist that their Eurocentric theological propositions have more to do with their white social location and environment than with any revelation from God is to invite accusations of "just being angry." A white, liberal colleague once challenged me to speak gently to white people who had supported and voted for a cockalorum in hopes of lovingly raising their consciousness and not turning them against me for coming off as too angry. White people would have me smile and gently explain that every four days, five brown bodies perish on our southern borders due to death-causing immigration policies or that those who make it have their infants and children ripped from their arms with no assurance of being reunited. Not since the days of Jim and Jane Crow have such detrimental governmental policies been put into place against certain people of color with the express purpose of deterring others from doing the same thing. Once again, it is the victim of white supremacy who is responsible for the well-being of those complicit with my people's decimation. Am I, a person of color, expected to meekly approach the master's table and politely discuss the nature of which particular scraps that have fallen to the floor might be available for me to gratefully devour? Yet in the face of policies designed to eradicate us, I am expected to be nice, mild, loving, and encouraging. With the boot of voter suppression on our necks, with a Justice Department determined to swell private prison corporations with bodies of color, with walls deigned to increase desert litter with more of our remains, the solution for soothing white distress rests upon the shoulders of those victimized.

To occupy a body of color within the United States is a continuous challenge. Not a day passes when I am not reminded I'm an outsider and that the space I occupy was never intended for me. To occupy this space, I (and all people of color) am forced to be fluent in Eurocentric philosophy and theology. To reject the worldview of those who excluded the colonized, attempting to construct my theological view on my own cultural context, is to risk being dismissed as unscholarly or exotic. No institution of higher education within the United States would have granted me a PhD if I were not fluent in Hegel, Heidegger, or Habermas. And yet my white colleagues are deemed rigorous scholars without ever having to read Sor Juana Inés de la Cruz, José Martí, or Miguel de Unamuno. I must be fluent in Eurocentric thought *and* knowledgeable about the contributions made by scholars relegated to the underside of the academy. While this double-consciousness gives me a broader and more rigorous grasp of reality than my white colleagues have, still a large number of those colleagues insist that affirmative action was responsible for my professorship.

It should be no secret that some of the worst racists are usually white liberals. If truth be known, I fear the right-wing conservatives less; for it is the liberals and moderates who, with bleeding hearts, decry the injustices they see while insisting that any remedy must proceed in a lawful and orderly manner—the same law and order responsible for structural oppression. I usually prefer neoconservatives, because they already see me as a *bad hombre*. At least I can appreciate their honesty and am under no illusion as to what I can expect. But the micro-aggressions of my white colleagues inflict the small paper cuts that with time will cause me to bleed to death. And those whites who recognize and admit their lack of knowledge concerning my context simply expect me to become their private tutor. Part of white privilege is the expectation that those on the margins exist to serve the center, understood, in my case, as being at the beck and call of any whites who happen to be Latinx-curious at the moment.

An Unholy Alliance

For white privilege to be maintained, white ignorance must be sustained. Such ignorance is dangerous for it threatens our very democracy. Our way of life will not falter due to invading armies or foreign powers. Democracy will wane in the era of an electorate's incredulous appetite for conspiracy theories that seek saviors among demagogues—saviors who promise a return to family values and conservative political mandates masquerading as Christian values. The greatest menace facing the United States is the patriots who follow the white-identity populism of Trump—or of any other racist politician for that matter—because they advance shared ideological positions while excusing well-documented lies whose jargogled truths threaten our democratic order.

White Christians railed against the threat of dictators and tyrants when a black man sat in the Oval Office, mainly because he was the wrong man for nationalist Christians to pledge allegiance to. But if the right/white man (yes, man, not woman) were to occupy the highest office, then concerns about authoritarianism would cease to exist. Such a man could unravel the democratic fabric without eliciting a raised eyebrow. Trump has been deemed by Christian nationalists to be the white/right man to satisfy their political yearnings, contributing to their concupiscence for a strong, dominating leader who would prompt unconditional submissive support in exchange for recreating the United States in their image.

Eurocentric Christianity has always been incongruent with democratic principles. While unfounded fears of the imposition of Sharia law haunt Islamophobic Christians, they have no reservations about imposing their own version of ancient scriptural commandments and regulations to create a Christian theocracy. Christian nationalism has never been comfortable with secular laws, especially secular laws that protect and promote basic human rights for those who fall outside the white Christian collective. Eurocentric Christian nationalism is fundamentally a nondemocratic ideological movement that rejects secular laws whenever its adherents believe those laws conflict with their interpretations of the laws of God. Because secular laws do not apply to them, they demand the right not to bake a wedding cake for a gay couple, or to fill a birth-control prescription for a sexually active woman, or even to allow people to have abortions.

A 2018 academic study discovered that while the vast majority of United States citizens support democratic rule, still nearly a quarter of all Americans prefer a strong leader who should not bother with Congress or elections, and more than a quarter support either a "strong leader" or "army rule." Those more likely to support authoritarian leadership describe themselves as "disaffected, disengaged from politics, deeply distrustful of experts [the educated], culturally conservative, and [holding] negative views toward racial minorities."[1] Not surprisingly, most of those who support authoritarian political systems were among those who supported Trump during the 2016 presidential primaries. And while the study did not explore the connection, if any, between religion and a desire for authoritarian political rule, I argue that a correlation does exists between a nationalist Christianity based on an authoritarian God, an authoritarian minister, and an authoritarian head of household with a longing by these same white Christian voters for an authoritarian president.

Rejecting democratic rule, these Christian nationalists, unsurprisingly, provide unwavering support for Trump, seeing his undemocratic policies and actions as necessary to bring about their beloved Christian nation. Such actions include:

1. Abdicating democratic moral authority by praising international bullies.

Admiration for authoritarian leaders is reinforced by Trump's feudatory pining for rising strongmen like Vladimir Putin of Russia, Viktor Orban of Hungary (whom Trump praised as "strong and brave"), Rodrigo Duterte of the Philippines, and more recently, Kim Jong-un of North Korea. And even though Trump may have joked about the United States following Xi Jinping's lead by declaring himself president for life, such comments are no laughing matter. The proposition is not funny because many white Christians would not mind having a president for life as long as that individual would promote and impose the agenda of Eurocentric Christianity. Entertaining such nondemocratic principles— even if jokingly—facilitates the rise of global fascist political movements.

2. Delegitimizing the free press.

According to this pugilistic president, "It is frankly disgusting the way the press is able to write whatever they want to write."[2] Nationalist Christians also find the free press disgusting because of its secular, so-called liberal bent. But the bedrock of safeguarding democracy has always been a free press. And while journalism does not always live up to its ideals and rhetoric, nonetheless it provides information so the populace can make informed decisions. Trump's rants of "fake news" about articles that hold him and his administration responsible for wrongdoings contribute to the weakening of the concept of truth. Following suit, Euro-American Christians also participate in ridiculing a media that for decades they have viewed as hostile to their understanding of faith.

3. Vilifying immigrants.

Even though it was reported in March 2018 that border-crossings were at their lowest rate since 1971, Trump nonetheless perpetuated the fearmongering propaganda of *Fox & Friends* that caravans of dangerous brown people were inching their way toward our borders. Mobilizing the National Guard to protect borders was simply political theater designed to give the illusion of protecting whites from imaginary brown threats. Former presidents George W. Bush and Barack Obama also engaged in this form of political grandstanding. Both sent the National Guard to the borders—Bush sending six thousand troops in 2006 and Obama sending twelve hundred in 2010 —in failed efforts to convince the Republican Congress that border security was being taken seriously. They hoped their symbolic tough stance on border security would entice Congress to pass a comprehensive immigration bill. Congress did not. What makes Trump's call for the National Guard different, and more cynical, is that he is propagating fear by demonizing brown gang members, whom he called animals—a fear that must be maintained at hysterically pitched levels if conservatives wish to motivate the gullible to vote in upcoming elections.

4. Neutralizing independent oversight by overriding constitutional checks and balances in the name of the people.

The president's attacks on the judicial system, on the FBI, and on the independent counsel investigating him undermine democratic safeguards. He couples these disturbing behaviors with a disregard for the rule of law by advocating and endorsing police brutality and questioning the integrity of the voting booth because he failed to win the popular vote.[3] If the president, any president, can do no wrong, we are perilously creeping toward an authoritarianism that frames democracy as the enemy of the people.

5. Demonizing loyal opposition.

When Democrats refused to applaud during Trump's 2018 State of the Union address, he referred to them as "un-American" and "treasonous."[4] Let's forget, for the moment, that Republicans did not find it necessary to applaud during Obama's speeches or that he was heckled by a Congressman who shouted "you lie."[5] In a democratic system, disagreement is not treason. It is only treason in authoritarian political structures.

Bringing a vision of a so-called Christ-centered nation to fruition is paramount; thus, white Christian nationalists really do not care whether Trump is a self-absorbed swindler (take, for example, Trump University) or a crude braggart who boasts about his adulteries and sexual assaults on women. What matters is the establishment of a so-called Christian nation. A 2018 sociological study showed that voting for Trump was, for many, a symbolic act in defense of some type of Christian heritage. The best predictor of who would vote for Trump was strong adherence to a Christian nationalist ideology—even after controlling for racism, sexism, Islamophobia, or political identity. The study concludes that "Christian nationalism operates as a unique and independent ideology that can influence political actions by calling forth a defense of mythological narratives about America's distinctively Christian heritage and future."[6] This Christian nationalism does not care about Trump's lack of Christian values or his authoritarian tendencies because their very mission—to claim the United States for the white Jesus—supersedes any fidelity to democratic principles or the rule of law. Ironically, Christian nationalists may think they are using (or God is using) Trump to achieve the theocracy of which they dream. But maybe it is Trump who is using them to satisfy his narcissism.

Oppressing Whites

If whites are angry, then they need to redirect their anger toward the social structures responsible for their economic predicament and those who benefit from such social structures. White Christians, hoping to convert America for Jesus, have chosen to dance with the perils that result from making alliances with those who benefit from their economic repression. For pledged privileges, they make an alliance with their richer compatriots, the 1 percent of whites who control 39 percent of the nation's wealth. They are played by their wealthier, colorblind counterparts, who could not care less about the skin pigmentation of those whom they, like hungry wolves, devour as long as profits can be maintained. Some naively seek to replay the Confederate heritage of dirt-poor whites who fought and offered up their lives to protect the slaveholders' privilege of owning human chattel. A small, wealthy cabal of whites bamboozle their skin-folk to embrace a kinship that provides the illusion of privilege to those sinking into financial and political despair. Rather than focusing on the actual causes for the downward mobility of the middle class, poorer whites redirect their wrath to those outside the realm of whiteness. White subservience to white privilege has always been a crucial ingredient in protecting and preserving the concentration of wealth and power in the hands of the very few.

Some might question my accusations against white privilege when they face the reality of financial struggles to make ends meet. Poor whites living paycheck-to-paycheck, fearing their jobs might be shipped south of the border, probably wonder, where is this power and privilege we supposedly possess? How does white privilege, therefore, privilege whites when their children are destined to be financially worse off than they are? As I said before, the words *white* and *whiteness* have less to do with skin pigmentation and more to do with a philosophical alliance to a power structure that privileges a small percentage of individuals. Some within communities of color who serve at the highest echelons of business and government also benefit from white privilege, just as there are plenty of individuals with lighter hues who recognize how they, too, are oppressed by white privilege. The downward economic spiral of the white middle class over the past five decades, along with the lingering consequences of the 2008 Great Recession caused by reckless, profiteering banking practices, has devastated not only communities of color but also the financial security of many whites. The "forgotten Americans"—the "white," forgotten Americans—cannot continue to be ignored because of their skin pigmentation. They too have suffered under white privilege.

Neoliberalism is colorblind. White, black, brown, red, and yellow shed blood of the same color when they are cut by the same blade of the global economy. Skin color—white, black, brown, red, and yellow—makes no difference to those who extract the green from the pockets of the dispossessed. White, black, brown, red, and yellow share the same disenfranchised space but are separated and divided from each other to ensure financial security for the privileged few. In a nation drunk with xenophobic madness, it is at times difficult to recognize that some whites are also being oppressed. All people in the United States' middle class, including whites, work longer hours and make less money when compared to their counterparts in Japan and Europe.

Thanks to the successes of Franklin Roosevelt's New Deal—currently threatened by Trumpist stalwarts— only one-fifth of families were in the lowest earning quintile by 1949, restoring levels to pre-Depression times. The 1950s witnessed a tremendous drop in poverty levels as median family income rose 43 percent higher by decade's end. Rather than crediting this to the New Deal, conservatives instead insisted this prosperity was the result of the post-war economy and women leaving the workforce to return home to bake cookies. Thus, if we hope to prosper, we need another war and a return to sexist and conservative family values. Unfortunately, Reaganomics reversed the economic gains made by the upwardly mobile middle class by dramatically widening the income gap and shrinking the middle class. During Reagan's presidency, the top 1 percent increased their earnings by 50 percent at the expense of the bottom 80 percent. At the beginning of his administration, the income of the top 1 percent was 65 times greater than that of the bottom 10 percent. By the end of his administration, their income was 115 times greater. While real income rose for all segments of society from 1947 through 1979, since 1980, income has *only* and consistently risen for the most affluent families.

Even during the 1990s, the economic boom that produced a six-trillion-dollar surplus benefited only the top quintile, increasing their share of the income. At the same time, the United States—according to the Congressional Budget Office—experienced the greatest wage inequality known throughout the Western world. The poor and middle class were excluded from the economic boom of the 1990s. Not since the Great Depression has the median family income dropped as substantially as it did throughout the first decade of the millennium under a presidency that squandered that six-trillion-dollar surplus. By 2012, during the first full year of the so-called recovery from the 2008 Great Recession, 93 percent of income gains went to the top 1 percent while 7 percent went to the remaining 99 percent.[7]

More and more whites found themselves slipping into greater poverty. As the doomed white middle class continued their downward slide, to whom did they look to blame? Was it those from the economically privileged segments of society who place short-term gains before the financial health of the nation? No, the middle class became some of the fiercest defenders of those profiting off their losses. Why would whites support governmental policies committed to a reverse Robin Hood? With a collective yawn, whites cheered as a 2017 tax bill gouged a collective $5.3 billion from those earning less than $50 thousand, in order for those earning a million or more to collect a combined $5.8 billion tax cut.[8] Like lambs being led to the slaughter, ignorance passively bleats while watching a trillion dollars added to the national debt. The only remedy to an expanding deficit caused by the 2017 tax cuts will be to further unravel the economic safety net through proposed and promised cuts in Medicare and Social Security. White Christians elect and support politicians who are detrimental to their own well-being. Bought and swapped like baseball trading cards by wealthier whites, these politicians may give the impression when they campaign that all white lives matter, but their actions reveal that certain white lives matter more than others.

The mood of a shrinking middle class is worrisome. In their minds, the failure for economic growth to occur in all strata of the population is not the fault of the top 1 percent; it is the fault of those who live outside of whiteness. Blame—like manure—flows downhill. The reasons offered by Fox News for white financial stress and distress are those "illegals" taking our jobs and welfare queens living off public assistance. The racism of these news outlets is redefined as patriotism. Whiteness becomes a sense of nationalist identity, a sense of community. Those who do not belong to the Euro-American community are thus responsible for its shortcomings because of their criticism of white identity. Those racially or ethnically identified outside a white community are set in opposition to the downwardly mobile white middle class. Those benefiting from the economic arrangement, the 1 percent and their managerial class, present disenfranchised communities of color as a wedge, a scapegoat to simplistically explain why whites are falling short of economic success.

Oppressed whites cling to an illusion of white identity and community that is constructed by the 1 percent to muffle cries for justice from the disinherited and dispossessed. And yet, whites excluded from the spaces occupied by the uber-wealthy have more in common with poor and middle-class communities of color than with their better-off white counterparts. Once white affirmative action, which eliminated competition from better qualified people of color, began to be dismantled, a whitelash swept into power those promising to make America White Again. Blaming those outside of whiteness for whites' economic distress creates an illusion that it is better to be poor and white than to be a middle-class person of color. Alt-right politicians and pundits are adept at manipulating racism to turn natural allies into mortal enemies. Racism trumps classism. Embracing a version, albeit weakened, of white identity, the white poor and middle class vote against their own economic self-interest. They embrace the laughable Laffer Curve—a theory that explains the relationship between taxes and government revenue—and thereby contribute to the plunder of their security and condemn themselves to greater destitution. Downplaying their financial hardships, some whites refuse to focus on the causes of their spiraling downward mobility.

Those lacking economic privilege, as my colleague John Raines reminds us, are taught to "dream up and blame down." As middle-class whites lose their financial footing, they continue to hold on to the false American dream of becoming wealthy and associating with society's elite. Empirical economic evidence confirms that the American dream, understood as the ability to become middle class through hard work and perseverance, exists only in rhetoric. For the past forty years, ascending to the next economic stratum above that in which one is born borders on the impossible. Failing to climb to the next class level, whites neither blame themselves nor the 1 percent for their economic collapse. Instead, they pass the blame downward, accusing those who are marginalized of stealing their jobs and depressing wages and thus preventing the true heirs of the American dream from achieving their rightful place in society.

This is why a black man elected president, or a woman running for the same office, faces such vehement resistance. This also might explain why when a Latino speaking in defense of white privilege throws his hat into the ring, he is embraced by the Republican Party as the great brown hope. Rather than looking up toward the 1 percent responsible for the growing wealth gap, thanks to their pocketful of senators, whites believe their representatives when they tell them that the real threats to their way of life are those who have historically been (and continue to be) outside whiteness. In other words, "Vote for me and I'll pass legislation, under the guise of religious freedom, if need be, to protect you from inferior and immoral people of darker shades of color who threaten your rightful place."

Those who benefit from the upward transfer of wealth wield tremendous political power and shape a false reality that absolves them of any complicity. "Make America Great Again" has become code language for suppressing the advancement and votes of nonwhites in the sincere belief that white supremacy would lead to greater privileges for all. Rather than looking to Wall Street and corporate interests, the white working-class blames their economic downward slide on the alien among us, the religious other, and people of color, who, they believe, are draining the system. The idea of reverse discrimination, used to explain why whites are getting such a raw deal—even though no empirical data exist to prove its existence—provides neat and simplistic explanations as to why whites are the true disadvantaged victims.

Racism and white supremacy are not inherited biases; they are philosophical ideologies created by a small, economically privileged group whose racist explanations are bescumbered upon an economically downward-spiraling white middle class. In spite of social and income stratification, racism and white supremacy provide false hope to the middle class that they too, if they are smart enough, if they keep their nose to the grindstone, or if they are favored by God, can join the rich and powerful; even though ascending to the highest echelons of economic privilege has more to do with an accident of birth than any other factor. Joe Lunchbucket is pacified knowing that regardless of how bad things might be, at least he is not black or Latinx. He may have difficulty paying a mortgage, but at least he has a mortgage to pay. Racism and white supremacy provide him with the reason he is struggling. Joe Lunchbucket, who probably doesn't have a racist bone in his body, as he is quick to remind us, nevertheless embraces racism and white supremacy because they give him someone else to blame for his economic predicament, providing a group upon whom to focus his fury and righteous indignation. Joe Lunchbucket becomes the forgotten American whom Trump and his ilk targeted, presenting themselves as ethnonationalist saviors, even though they made their riches swindling Joe out of fair wages and social services.

But even if Joe Lunchbucket had marched with Martin Luther King Jr. or once dated a Latina in college, he is still a racist because he benefits from racist structures designed to provide him with the illusion of, and at times actual, privilege over and against those with darker skins. Racism has nothing to do with biases. Racism means complicity with the social structures that are racist for Joe. The tragedy is that the supposed saviors of the white middle class and poor whites are colorblind skin-folk. Those who rigged the economic structures to capture 93 percent of all income gains since the Great Recession become the hope of poorer whites. Never mind that the recession from which they profited financially set white middle-class Euro-Americans back a generation or two. If truth be told, the salvation of whites lies with those very people they been taught to blame and hate for their economic situation.

Subverting White Supremacy

Historically, white Euro-Americans have shed the blood of darker bodies so they might have life and have it more abundantly. The marginalized are offered up as living sacrifices to the God of white Christianity. Quite frankly, the rise of the United States had less to do with God's favor or the superior intellect of white people than the fact that the United States' wealth, global power, and place in the world as the greatest empire ever known, are due to those who have been crucified in her name. America's greatness would never have risen to its present level if not for the stolen land of indigenous people, the free slave labor of black bodies, and the twentieth-century invasions into countries of Latinxs' origins to steal their land, their raw materials, and their cheap labor. America was made great through the exploitation and subjugation of those who fell short of the white ideal, an exploitation and subjugation masked as God's favor toward God's new chosen people. White Christianity must be created and constructed to religiously justify theft and rape as God's will. Most communities of color feel a chill running up their collective spine whenever white folk, ignorant of their own history, chant the need to "Make America Great Again" because those of us who carry the stigmata of United States' history know all too well how the grinding of our forebear's lives and the crushing of their bones into dust was the price paid for America's greatness.

The 1 percent who benefit from the status quo of divide-and-conquer are actually afraid of a future in which society truly moves to reject racism and white supremacy. They fear poor and middle-class whites might join forces with communities of color to demand justice to roll down like living water and righteousness to flow like an everlasting stream! White solidarity with those they have historically blamed can provide whites with liberation from the misguided faith they have and continue to place in their wealthier and whiter counterparts. This explains how the notion of MAGA allows for the divisive actions of Charlottesville's goose-steppers who call for *Blut und Boden* (blood and soil), the purification of white blood to occupy the Promised Land at the expense of the red blood flowing through everyone else's veins. But they can never be washed clean in the blood of the lambs they slaughter! Salvation, for their own souls and for the nation's, can occur only through the crucifixion of whiteness. However, as long as white supremacy continues to exist and thwart the efforts of coalition-building for a more just society, the 1 percent can continue to hold the reins of power.

This is not the first time the dominant culture has fostered division between marginalized groups to secure its hold on society. Racism and white supremacy are strategies older than this nation. Virginia elites during colonial times learned they could better secure their aristocratic space by forcing those who could have been natural allies against their rule to compete against each other for scraps. These noble whites succeeded in preventing allegiances from developing between the two oppressed groups of their time, slaves (blacks) and former indentured servants (poor whites), by endowing the latter with certain privileges at the expense of the former. Prior to 1670, little difference in living conditions existed between poor white indentured servants, considered "the scruff and scum of England," and black slaves, considered mere possessions. As more slaves flooded the colonies, an economic shift developed from a white indentured servitude-based economy where poor whites worked for a limited number of years, to a slave-based economy where Africans, although costing twice as much as poor whites, worked, along with their progeny, the entirety of their lives. In 1676, poor whites and black slaves joined forces in armed revolt against economic injustice. The Bacon Rebellion created unity among the economically oppressed, disrupting and threatening the ruling class. A band of brothers (and sisters) was created among whites and blacks as their blood spilled, mixed, and flowed on the streets of Jamestown, their bodies joined as one in the grip of death.

Colonial Virginia's 1 percent learned its lesson all too well. If poor whites formed alliances with oppressed blacks, the 1 percent's rule as elites would be vulnerable. Precautions against such alliances were woven into the very fabric of what would emerge a century later as a new republic. Fear of future rebellions and a changing economic base led Virginia's "*crème de la crème*" to pass legislation (the Virginia Slave Codes of

1704) that created social divisions between blacks and poor whites through a racial caste system in order to secure the 1 percent a privileged place in the emerging nation. Poor whites received a pittance of privilege at the expense of their former black allies in exchange for loyalty to the reigning economic oppressors. An economic strategy emerged that has served the privileged class well for the rest of this country's history, a strategy still operating specifically in today's economic environment.

Liberation for whites requires that they engage in a deeper analysis of how the prevailing economic forces of neoliberalism are pauperizing them, as they have always impoverished those who are not white. If white consciousness can be raised, alliances might be reformed. Creating economic pacts between former racial adversaries, however, can be deadly. If Martin Luther King Jr. had not turned his attention to the Poor People's March, bringing together bodies representing the rainbow of humanity, united by their shared poverty, he might very well have died of old age. For economically oppressed whites to march with people of color is too dangerous for those economically privileged by whiteness. How is it possible, then, to make even the likelihood of co-operation among economically disadvantaged groups abhorrent? If such an alliance were attempted, we could expect that every tool at the disposal of the 1 percent—politicians, media, police, courts, military—would be expended to prevent such a coalition. Accusations of "class warfare" (the very opposite of a coalition strategy) would saturate the discourse. The best way to keep whites docile is by creating a spiritual response to poverty, a response that blames the victim of economical oppression and not their oppressors.

Since the days of John Calvin, when a theology of election was articulated, the church has sought to distinguish the saved from the damned. If God chooses the saved, and if salvation does not depend on human actions or decisions, then how do we know who is among the elect? We know who is saved because God blesses God's chosen. A Protestant work ethic is developed, according to Max Weber, that becomes a crucial force behind the uncoordinated rise of capitalism. As some of these Calvinists became wealthy, especially those in New England, who profited from and thus justified slavery and the slave trade, they looked to God as the source of their riches and proof of their sanctification, instead of the profits they extracted, along with the blood and sweat, from the business of buying and selling human beings. No greater proof was needed of Africans not being chosen by God than the fact they suffered under white oppression.

Even today, when we come across a street person, regardless of her or his race, many of us, influenced by simplistic Calvinist thought, tend to blame the victim of neoliberalism for her or his homelessness. We rationalize that homeless people are probably alcoholics or drug users—and if only they knew Jesus they wouldn't be in this predicament. More important than meeting their physical needs is ensuring their spiritual salvation. As the nineteenth-century evangelist Dwight Moody observed:

> My idea was that I could open a poor man's heart by giving him a load of wood or a ton of coal when the winter was coming on, but I soon found out that he wasn't any more interested in the gospel on that account. Instead of thinking how he could come to Christ, he was thinking how long it would be before he got the load of wood. If I had the Bible in one hand and a loaf [of bread] in the other the people always looked first at the loaf; and that was just the contrary of the order laid down in the Gospel.[9]

Advocating social justice—feeding the hungry—has nothing to do with white Christianity. Any attempt at transforming society to be more just requires decentering the efforts of evangelizing poor whites with the gospel of white privilege obtained through a white Jesus.

Reading the Gospel of Mark, Not Marx

Televangelist Jesse Duplantis, who has been accused of violating tax laws to fund his extravagant lifestyle, has asked the faithful to donate $54 million to his ministry so he can purchase a Falcon 7X jet, which would allow him to "go anywhere in the world in one stop" to preach the gospel of Jesus Christ. This new jet would replace the one he already has. God, to whom he has referred as a "sugar daddy," will provide. Of course, he is not alone. Kenneth Copeland asked for $17 million in donations to upgrade his Gulfstream V jet.[10] An unholy union exists between some white Christians and a religious justification for enriching oneself. Following the prosperity gospel justifies multimillionaire charlatans who wear consecrated vestments made of sheep's clothing in obtaining a certain level of earthly riches never promised by the one in whose name they slaughter the hungry, thirsty, naked, and the alien within our midst. The apostate name-it-and-claim-it belief, which validates mansion-owning preachers flying private jets paid for by the widow's mite as the will of God, is an abomination before all that is holy.

Coming to prominence during the 1950s, this prosperity gospel provided spiritual justification for the uncritical amassment of wealth, relieving unscrupulous Euro-American Christians and their descendants of guilt or shame over how their wealth was amassed. In their minds, they are rich not because they have the power to manipulate laws—specifically tax laws—but because they are faithful to a God who favors a Rome-America. And because God wills riches for the heirs to the throne, those who are still mired in poverty serve as living proof that they live outside the will of God. Their own poverty condemns them. When we consider the historical racial caste system in the United States that is responsible for the wide wealth gap between whites and people of color, it must mean God loves and favors whites more, because they control more wealth, overall, than people of color.

The culture of the United States has learned to equate Christianity with capitalism and to define all other types of economic systems, using either neat dichotomies or a broad brush, as communist. Such a move accomplishes two tasks. First, it dismisses our ability to critique capitalism, because it has come to be confused with the very Word of God. Second, this type of reaction reveals the US culture's inability to distinguish real differences between authoritarian communism (North Korea), authoritarian socialism (Cuba, Venezuela), democratic socialism (Scandinavian countries), mixed economies (Iceland, the United Kingdom), authoritarian capitalism (Russia, China), and plutocratic capitalism (United States).

Within the United States, white Christians view the act of critiquing capitalism as an attack on their faith and a call for class warfare. Politicians and political pundits use the term "class warfare" whenever the public (rich or poor) begins to question the disparity of wealth in this or any other nation. To raise concerns about the ever-growing wealth gap within the United States is to risk being accused of fomenting social unrest, or worse, being labeled a socialist. When Warren Buffet, a billionaire capitalist, contemplated why he pays a lower tax rate than his secretary, Fox News pundit Eric Bolling labeled him a socialist. As much as we may wish to avoid the term "class warfare," lest we too be called socialist—as if the term "socialist" is synonymous with the satanic—the truth remains that class warfare is currently being waged by politicians who are protecting the super-rich. They are winning! And here is the irony. The capitalism (or better yet, neoliberalism) that has been implemented in the United States in its Reaganomics form has become a threat to a capitalism based on entrepreneurship, as resources continue to be concentrated in fewer hands. Just notice how many mom-and-pop shops close once Walmart moves into a neighborhood. Such concentration of resources eliminates economic competition, suppresses wages, and enriches the few. Corporate mergers and the proliferation of acquisitions enabled by deregulation are more effectively destroying capitalism than any communist could ever dream of doing.

This capitalism/neoliberalism, which has developed since the 1980s, is a major threat to democracy in the United States as "one person-one vote" is replaced with "one dollar-one vote." "Corporations are people too," we are told. The Supreme Court's decision equating multinational corporations with citizens and massive political contributions (bribes?) with free speech has effectively reinforced the golden rule—"the one with the gold makes the rules." Capitalism may resonate with Christian nationalists, but its fundamental principles are antithetical to true Christianity. The basic thesis of Adam Smith in *Wealth of Nations* is that individuals should be allowed and encouraged to pursue self-interests. "It is not from the benevolence of the butcher, the brewer, or the baker, that we expect our dinner, but from their regard to their own self-interest"[11] By doing so, all society will benefit, says Smith. But for those who are Christians, the Gospels teach us to place the needs and interests of others before our own. Hence an internal contradiction and an irreconcilable difference exist between capitalism and Christianity. How does one place one's own self-interests first (capitalism) while putting the interest of others first (Christianity)? Such a divided house cannot stand. Rather than being afraid of accusations of class warfare, it might be wiser to embrace the "socialist" label by resisting the class warfare brought to our front door thanks to Reaganomics.

More than 41 percent of all global personal wealth is concentrated in the United States (the country with the next-largest share is China with a little over 10 percent). The United States, with over $63 trillion in total private wealth, making it the richest empire on earth, also has the largest wealth-inequality gap among the richest fifty-five nations. For these reasons, Pope John Paul II believed that our "savage capitalism" was fundamentally non-Christian. The vast majority of whites who suffer at the hands of savage capitalism dream upward, duped into forming allegiances with a smaller, wealthier, and whiter contingency who profit by their downward slide. Then, the whites who don't succeed blame downward, choosing racist ideologies to provide simplistic answers to their financial predicament. The fallacy of whiteness lies in scorning natural allies in favor of the illusion of power and privilege.

The Seduction of White Women

I have found some white women more resistant to strategic alliances than some white men. I have found that white, female colleagues are fearful of confident men of color, preferring servile subordinates who reinforce their white privilege. Chicana Cherríe Moraga observes that white feminists seldom analyze how the very nature and structure of their group itself may be founded on racist or classist assumptions. White supremacy in the United States has been seen, defined, and understood as a male-focused venture. From once wearing the white sheets of anonymity and riding on horseback into the night with flaming crosses to terrorize black families to now wearing white polo shirts and carrying tiki torches on college campuses, men have been the foot soldiers of the race-based movement. Patriarchal pastors preached a Klan-friendly Christianity that emphasized the curse of Ham, while elite politicians legislated a Christian-based Jim and Jane Crow at the city council, in the state house, in Congress, and in the White House. Missing from the overarching racist narrative is the role white women play, the white women who washed and ironed those white sheets then or who don white polo shirts now. Missing from the historical narrative are the unnamed women who, as school teachers, church ladies, midwives, and socialites, protected their children from the perceived menace of those who would sully genteel, white purity. These white women, who today are senators, CEOs, and university presidents, have betrayed and continue to betray gender equality because of the central role they play in perpetuating the same racist policies of their male counterparts.

Abused white women have been used (and have used each other) to instigate and justify violence against black and brown men. While I applaud white women's courage for coming forth during the #MeToo movement to out the pervasiveness of sexual assault and harassment they faced every single day, men of color remain haunted by false accusations proven deadly as demonstrated by commonplace "rascal lynchings" during Jim and Jane Crow for "outraging [raping] a white woman." Cases like the Scottsboro boys, the Groveland Four, the Spell trial, and, of course, Emmett Luis Till, prove that white women's lies matter. Entire cities were leveled because of false accusations against men of color, such as the Omaha Riot (1891: unknown number dead), the Atlanta Race Riots (1906: 100 dead), the Tulsa Race Riots (1921: 300 dead), and the Rosewood Massacre (1923: 150 dead), to name but a few. A long history of false allegations, whose origins can be traced to the first black man disembarking on these shores in chains, is not relegated to historical footnotes as Leiha Ann-Sue Artman (2016) or Breana Harmon Talbott (2017), who each falsely accused men of color of raping them, recently demonstrated. False accusations made out of fear of dark men, a persistent stereotype designed to dehumanize, is the ignored part of the #MeToo discourse. White men projected their uncontrollable libidos upon those with darker skin pigmentation to divert their own predatory lust while providing permission to discipline men of color as soon as a white woman expressed her fear. This is not to excuse or ignore the sexual predatory practices also present among men of color, but rather to deepen the discourse by highlighting the historical role white women's complicity with racism has played. White women have more to fear from their white counterparts than from men of other races. White women are more vulnerable in the presence of President Trump than in that of Jesús the building custodian. And yet, they have been taught since childhood to fear Jesús and not Donald.

One would think white, liberal women would be natural allies with communities of color. After all, they have experienced millennia of sexism and sexual abuse. Betraying their ability to prioritize gender inequality as a self-delusion, they envision themselves as the white messiahs of women of color whom they perceive as suffering under a worse form of gender oppression based on the assumption men of color are somehow more sexist and beastly than white men. Note: all forms of sexism are devastating to all women—no racial or ethnic group has a monopoly on misogyny, no single racial or ethnic group does sexism better or worse than another. While I recognize that occupying a male body makes me complicit with sexist social structures, I also remain keenly aware that a majority of white women support racist and homophobic institutionalized violence. As my white colleague Laura Striver reminds us, the middle- to upper-class white women promoting liberal feminism assumed that their needs mirrored the primary needs of all other women, blind to the ways race and class, not simply gender, shaped women's experiences.

Many white women place their race privilege over and against gender issues, maybe as a form of survival within a sexist society, maybe as an attempt to position themselves on a higher rung of the hierarchal, oppressive social structure. Fidelity to whiteness trumps the injustice of sexism. Sexual inequality and abuse at the hands of white men is preferable to the fear that qualified men or women of color may surpass them in the white-imposed national hierarchy. No greater proof exists of the betrayal of feminist ideals than the majority of white women—53 percent—who voted for a known sexual predator who bragged about grabbing women by their pussies. And before we dismiss these women as simply being ignorant or uneducated, we do well to remember that 44 percent of them had attended college! Worse are the 63 percent of white women who voted for a child-molester in order to maintain a Republican majority in the Senate. Black women in Alabama believed the testimonies of white teenaged girls who were preyed upon at the local mall by the then-assistant district attorney, more so than the white women who turned their backs on their younger skin-folk sisters by prioritizing political expedience. And yet, many of these same white women continue to envision themselves as the saviors of women of color!

Regardless of their protestations to the contrary, white women do not want to discuss race or ethnic discrimination. As my colleague Nichole Flores observes, conversations intended to focus on racial inequality always have a funny way of ending up focused on gender inequality.[12] Almost every person of color has experienced at least once how a white woman, with a single tear upon her lily-white cheek, can shift the focus of the discussion from exposing white women's complicity with racist structures to eliciting comfort for her feeling vulnerable upon the exposure of her racism and ethnic discrimination. White women are privileged by their economic class or protected by the cultural norm of white supremacy. The problem then is that most white women vote to uphold patriarchy to maximize their own power and privilege within a racially pluralistic society. Compare this to the 98 percent of black women who voted against alleged sexual predator Roy Moore in Alabama or the 91 percent who voted against Trump in 2016, as well as the 68 percent of Latinas who also rejected the predator-in-chief. As long as white women continue to monopolize the feminist conversation, no advances will be made in favor of gender equality in this country. The feminist cause would be better served if white women were willing to set aside their own notions of what is best and instead listen to, learn from, and follow the lead of black women and Latinas who have rejected the white nationalism white women continue to embrace.

Like poor whites who dream upward but blame downward, most white women voters support patriarchy because they define reality through the eyes of white, Christian men who accept as natural their God-ordained place within society. Patriarchy benefits not only men, but also certain white women who avoid the semblance of overtly dismantling oppressive social structures by instead submitting and/or subjugating themselves to gain access and inclusion among those whom the structures actually privilege. Here lies the concern in any equality conversation among white men and white women where people of color are dismissed from the discourse. Is equality for women, and by extension people of color, achieved by ontologically becoming white males? Do white women achieve self-realization when they ascend to positions of power in government, the boardroom, and society? In other words, is liberation the act of becoming a white male with all the oppressive power and unearned privileges that have become part of male whiteness? Although white women had historically been relegated to positions of passiveness compared to male competitiveness, today's people of color, female and male, are relegated to the role white women had historically occupied. Women and men of color are the ones usually consigned to the trivial jobs and who earn a substandard living. Many white women have defined their liberation by becoming the new ontological white male, not just to the detriment of women and men of color, but also to themselves.

Bleaching Colored Folk

The fallacy of whiteness is not limited to white people. Crabbing was one of the ways the poor in Miami got to eat. When my wife was a young girl, her family would visit the beach to hunt crabs. She became adept at finding her prey and placing it in a white plastic bucket. Later, at home, her *abuela* would prepare them for dinner, thus stretching their food budget. On the drive home, she had a crucial task—to watch the bucket lest a crab attempt a getaway. Surprisingly, few ever escaped, for every time a crab climbed to the top rim of the bucket, one of those below would pinch the would-be fugitive's leg and drag it back down. Historically oppressed groups at times behave like the bucket of crabs, liable for their own oppression. We are at times our worst enemies, selling out our communities for a seat at the master's table.

Crabs believe that in order to succeed they must make sure no one else in the zero-sum-rule white bucket can achieve new heights. And if any do, they should be punished and brought back down. People of color at times fulfill the stereotypes imposed by the dominant culture, concerned more with protecting their "turf" or "recognized" status within the disenfranchised community than with protecting the rights of our people. The bucket-of-crabs analogy is extended when those who achieve some measure of success embrace whiteness, turning their backs on their own community by refusing to reinvest their talents and resources in others who are disenfranchised.

The best way to maintain oppression is for the oppressed to embrace white Christianity. While I appreciate white allies willing to stand in solidarity with us, I remain troubled when communities of color refuse to define and implement their own process of liberation, instead choosing to define their struggle through the very white Christian concepts responsible for their oppression. There is power in defining words. Whites have the power to transform concepts like "justice" and "liberation" into repulsive expressions used to perpetuate the colonization of the minds of those relegated to inferior status. A mind liberated from its colonial manacles can become fertile ground from which sprouts resistance to the dominant worldview constructed to sustain white privilege. But as long as concepts like "justice" and "liberation" are defined by the dominant white culture, we will never achieve deliverance from oppressive structures. White gatekeepers can always find some religious leader with a "colored" face who can be placed on some pedestal to sing the praises of Trump's divisive, bigoted populism and the colonializing Christianity he advocates. Some Judas can always be found to do the dirty work of those wanting to protect white power and privilege. Priestly leadership rejoiced when one of Jesus's own came forward to spew lies and allegations.

As my colleague Stacey Floyd-Thomas constantly reminds us: "Not all skin-folk are kinfolk, and not all kin are kind." There are always those from marginalized communities who are willing to put on white masks, for survival or profit, willing to be the henchmen and henchwomen of white supremacy. The hands of these self-appointed spokespersons are too stained with the blood of our people to ever be part of our quest for liberation. Our freedom and dignity are traded for the political gain of a few crabs. These are the faces of color who regularly appear on Fox News, using their white voices to defend the status quo. Here's a clue: if white Christians in the United States are singing your praises, then you might be a tool and a danger to your own community. And the sad reality is that your mind might be so colonized—as my own mind was—that you might not even be aware of the damage being done.

If white supremacy is sustained and maintained by ignorance, then be aware that you have just read a testimony from the underside of white privilege. You can no longer claim ignorance or disregard your complicity with white Christianity. Here's another funny thing about crabs. In their natural habitat, they pull each other up to the safety of rocks as ocean waves come crashing down. The white bucket is not their natural habitat–the rocks are. The crabs in a bucket act against their own best interest because they are placed in an artificially oppressive environment. Liberation from Euro-centric Christianity as manifested by conservatives and liberals must begin with disenfranchised communities seeking the decolonization of their minds, understanding they have been placed in a white bucket constructed to ensure that, as crabs, they see themselves through the eyes of their captors, and thus impose upon themselves and their fellow crabs their own discipline. And while white allies are always welcomed to assist in kicking over the white bucket, they are welcomed to follow—but never lead. Enough with white Christians and their messianic complexes!

3

Maintaining and Sustaining Self-Deception

Some white Christians voted for Trump out of a profound dislike for his political rival Hillary Clinton. Others claimed they voted for him because they believed in his vision of "Making America Great Again" or because he promised the country would "tire of so much winning." Maybe some voted for a pro-life Trump because he vowed to safeguard the Supreme Court from liberal entrenchment by making conservative appointees. And still others might have believed a pragmatic businessman in the Oval Office would be good for the country. Yet Christian nationalists continue to be his most ardent supporters due to the overt racism and ethnic discrimination he continues to exhibit, a racism made quite evident throughout the campaign season and his presidency.

Regardless of the apologetic reasons white Christians give for casting their lot with Trump, their true motive was their fear of Latinxs swarming over the border like cockroaches, Muslims seeking to enact Sharia law while carrying bombs under their burkas, black rapists lusting after white women, and a homosexual agenda that threatens traditional marriages by forcing everyone to be gay. Fear of the other and a patriotic desire to return to a simpler, more racist time had more to do with casting votes for Trump than the wish to fight against any politically correct alternative offered. White Christian nationalists may insist they too are horrified at Trump's actions, behavior, and tweets; yet, they continue to justify voting for an avowed misogynist racist by arguing they voted for a president not a preacher, and that God can use even the pagan Cyrus to bring about God's will. The not-so-secret reason as to why white Christians voted for and continue to support Trump was their desire to ensure the White House would be white again and would remain so for the forseeable future.

But to continue supporting Trump after his failure to condemn Nazi and Klan activities in Charlottesville is deeply troubling and reflects a national moral crisis. Support for Trump does not waver because Euro-American Christians are aligned—and historically have always been aligned—with his racist, white-nationalist viewpoint. To stand before the public, as Trump did, after a white man purposely drove his car into a group of peaceful protestors and say there is blame on many sides is to provide cover for white terrorist groups who are fueled by hatred for people of color and their allies (both right- and left-of-center) who stand with them. To say all sides are to blame ignores how only one side carried guns, while the other side wore clerical collars. One side chanted epithets toward Jews and blacks while the other side prayed for love and peace. Trump appealed to white Christian nationalists because of his explicit rhetoric of reinstituting and reinforcing white supremacy. If the president or his white Christian allies cannot bring themselves to condemn the perpetrators of home-grown terrorism, then both the president and his white Christian allies are racist. Yes, I know white people hate being called racist, but honestly, what other term best captures and explains this phenomenon? Embrace the term and repent, or simply prove me wrong. Not in words, but in deeds! Really there is only one way to disprove my thesis: condemn white supremacy in all its forms and manifestations without qualification, including its overwhelming prevalence in the Trump administration. Further, take accountable actions to ensure it is eradicated from our democratic society.

Nativism Trumps Self-Interest

Some liberals believe that sleeping with a Latino or a black woman while in college is enough to prove they are woke and progressive. Having Asian grandchildren does not give you a pass. Attending an Indian powwow falls way too short. Singing a hymn or two in Spanish, followed by a taco church supper is window-dressing. Complicity is proven by the deafening silence that follows modern-day brown shirts wearing white polo shirts who terrorized United States citizens. Milquetoast responses that all sides are to blame (reminiscent of how Nazis blamed Jews for Kristallnacht) simply make Eurocentric Christianity an ally, an enabler, and an advocate of Nazis, the Klan, and skinheads. Silent support for Charlottesville's white supremacists makes complicity a reality. White privilege employs the doublespeak of heritage-preservation while gaslighting opponents of antifascist movements as the purveyors of hatred. Jesus has not yet recovered from the vomiting induced by Christian defenders of torch-wielding white nationalists chanting, "Jews will not replace us."

I can't imagine how the man who blasts 280 characters against every minuscule slight cannot find even eight characters to condemn the obvious: N-a-z-i b-a-d. A man who bombarded both Barack Obama and Hillary Clinton for their refusal to say the words *Islamic Terrorism* cannot find the will to write *White Terrorism* (fifteen characters). The president and white Christians are quick to call it terrorism (as they should) when a Muslim drives a vehicle into a crowd, but when a white person does the same, this act is merely a civil disturbance? Or the act of a deranged lone wolf? For the record, of the hundreds of Muslims whom I know and collaborate with, not one has ever given me any cause to fear. I cannot say the same about the white people whom I know and with whom I collaborate.

Allow me to speak plainly. The mask has been ripped off to show the hatred and racism beneath the Trump façade. Our nation is divided. Our nation has a history of promoting hatred for the other. In the face of injustice, neutrality can never be an option. Silence makes the uncommitted bedfellows with hatred and racism—whether they like it or not. Our lack of humanity is defined by the refusal to condemn the alt-right white Christian nationalist movement and agenda. Our lack of humanity is defined by the willingness to serve as apologists for certified hate groups like the Family Research Council (according to the Southern Poverty Law Center) whose president, Tony Perkins, was tapped for a seat on the bipartisan International Religious Commission by US Senate Majority Leader Mitch McConnell.

But what seems obvious to the dispossessed and disinherited is obfuscated by coastal pundits, progressive politicians, and academic intellectual elites who bemoan their failure to fully grasp the plight and grievances of the so-called "forgotten Americans"—the hard-working, gun-toting, God-loving, economically struggling whites of the reddish flyover landscape. During his inaugural speech, Trump vowed to empower these whites, promising that "The forgotten men and women will be forgotten no more." Yes, they are frustrated and fed up, angry about the present and anxious about the future. And even though their ancestors also might have struggled economically, they at least clung to the promises of white supremacy. No matter how bad things might be, their forebears would always be better off than "them colored folk" and foreigners. But yesterday's privileges have become today's fallacies, because the color-blind 1 percent cares less about the hue of those from whom they squeeze the last drops of profit. White liberal America did not underestimate the forgotten American. They simply refused to provide the proper diagnoses of how racism, ethnic discrimination, and fear of the other leads to suspicion of the other, which in turn leads to hatred of the other, culminating in voting against one's own self-interest out of concern that the other will further erode their illusion of white supremacy. Fear, suspicion, and hatred are not characteristics of the uneducated alone; those with fancy abbreviations after their names are just as fearful, suspicious, and hatemongering.

David Norman Smith and Eric Allen Hanley, in their 2018 study published in *Critical Sociology*, debunked the reigning myth that the typical white who voted for Trump in 2016 was simply uneducated. By using multivariate logistic regression, they demonstrated that the primary motivation for the typical Trump supporter casting his or her vote was an attraction to his authoritarian style, which targeted women and minorities. They favored domineering and intolerant leaders uninhibited about their prejudices and biases. The researchers concluded the white Trump vote had more to do with shared prejudices than any personal financial stress they might have been experiencing. They were the "forgotten

Americans," not because they felt left out from the economic riches this country possesses, but because white power and privilege had ceased to be treasured commodities.[1] Whites were not forgotten because they were locked out of opportunities; they were forgotten because nonwhites were making advances thanks to the dismantling of an affirmative action that, since the founding of the country, had privileged whiteness over others. Unable to effectively vie with capable women and men of color on a fair and level playing field, they cling to white legacy rights in order to mute competition and ensure success. They find it easier to claim being a "forgotten American" than recognize their racism. Besides, claiming victimhood always sounds better than admitting one's failure when one is competing against those historically seen, defined, and legitimized as inferiors.

Blaming downward offers a tangible reason for their predicament, as well as an object upon which to unleash their fury. Blaming downward explains financial failures while masking the institutionalized biases of the downwardly mobile middle-class. The strategy of blaming marginalized communities diverts and transfers blame away from the shrinking community of economic elites, a strategy, as we saw, dating to colonial times. This national self-deception needs careful and continuous maintenance and sustenance, because if the opposite were true, and minorities were *not* to blame for whites falling short of economic success, then who or what is actually to blame? The alt-right, as well as the liberals who join them by refusing to consider what so many communities of color need little persuasion to accept, must therefore continue in this belief, while wearing its public cloak of color blindness. Failure to explore the fallacy of whiteness in its larger context, by dismissing the election of an avowed racist thanks to the votes cast by angry and forgotten citizens, will only ensure future elections of other Trumps.

When the Justice Department handed down charges against thirteen Russians and three companies for undermining the 2016 election that gave us a President Trump, it was interesting to note how the Russians had succeeded. They designed a sophisticated online network. Through stolen identities, they posed as activists to raise distrust, animosity, and division among the United States public. The Russians accomplished their goals by agitating the electorate with the hot-button issues of race, religion, and immigration, stoking the fear, suspicion, and hatred of white Christian nationalists. Specifically, they played to the loss of white supremacy in order to rally the so-called forgotten Americans into action. And while it may be true the Russians manipulated historical flashpoints, the fact remains that Trump is president because of the problem of whiteness and the cover provided by white Christianity in the United States, regardless of Russian meddling.

The Cult of Trump

The authoritarian, patriarchal Trump style is not a stranger to the Eurocentric Christian world. The Christian faith, in its political construction, was founded upon an authoritarian organization modeled on an authoritarian family unit. Just as the husband is the ordained head of the household, called by God to be a modern-day Abrahamic patriarch, so too are priests, called fathers, the ordained heads of churches. And while Protestants shy away from the word *father*, they nevertheless create similar authoritarian structures where congregants submit to a pastor who serves as the spiritual head. For centuries, even before the foundation of the republic, Eurocentric Christianity has legitimized a patriarchy where authoritarian men rule at home, rule in the church, and rule in public. The system of checks and balances in the US government becomes a nuisance to be dismantled instead of a safeguard designed to protect us from authoritarian rule. Further complicating patriarchy is the way in which whiteness expanded the authoritarian model by feminizing men and women of color, thus placing their fate under the benevolent masculine hand of the white, male overseer who knows what is best for inferior people. Christianity in the United States is simply simpatico with a political model designed to justify white supremacy.

When authoritarian figures can do no wrong, the problem is not so much with the leader but with the followers,

who, like followers of religious cults, willingly drink the proverbial Kool-Aid regardless of how high their IQ may actually
be. Seeing their unearned, privileged positions threatened
by merit-based concepts such as equality, they embrace cult
leaders who present themselves as the only solution to their
downward-spiraling predicament, or as Trump proclaimed
while mounting the Republican National Convention stage: "I
am your voice. I alone can fix it." Because only the cult leader
can save us, he can do no wrong. Mao, Stalin, or Castro from
the political left can do no wrong; Hitler, Mussolini, or Pi-
nochet from the political right can do no wrong; Jim Jones,
Marshall Applewhite, or David Koresh from the religious
fringes can do no wrong. And when leaders can do no wrong,
lemmings follow unto death.

During the presidential campaign, Trump bragged about
being able to shoot somebody in broad daylight in the middle
of Fifth Avenue and lose no voters. And the crowd cheered.
Trump can do no wrong. Even at Helsinki, he can stand in
agreement with Putin, betray his own intelligence agencies,
and do no wrong. The people transfer their absolute faith
in God to Trump. So, too, they redirect their unconditional
love from God to Trump. In an ultimate narcissistic move,
Trump replaces God in accepting what is due to the Deity and
in promising what the faithful can expect in return. If this is
not idolatry, then I don't know what is.

Steven Hassan, a former cult member and current clini-
cal professional dedicated to assisting and enfranchising cult

members, believes Trump fits the stereotypical profile of a cult leader. When Trump's followers continue to proclaim their fidelity ("He could do anything and we would still believe him, we will still follow him"), they reveal their total indoctrination into a totalistic mindset. Such a mindset can be maintained only by redefining reality.[2] Even though Trump was caught on tape bragging about grabbing women by their genitalia without their consent—a tape we actually heard with our own ears—Trump can nonetheless dismiss it as fake news and profess no one has more respect for women. "Believe me," he says, and they do.

Maybe Trump was simply a con artist when he was hustling nondescript apartments as the pinnacle of class and luxury or running a university scam that bilked many with promises of revealing the secrets to becoming rich. The con artist, fueled by a craving for approval and adulation, attracts followers who feed the narcissistic addiction to power, fame, money, and sex. Neither laws of nature nor human-made rules apply to cult leaders, for they appear to operate above the law. "Jokes" of following China's example of possibly having a president for life lose all humor when voiced by cult leaders. And here is the truly disturbing thing: the same people who opposed Obama for being, in their minds, an illegitimate president, a tyrant, and a dictator, embrace an illegitimate president who lost the popular election by almost three million votes and who has made no secret of his admiration for tyrants and dictators or of his desire to follow their example.

These gun-toting, white Christian defenders of liberty and the American way are democracy's current threat.

The Problem with Whiteness

If the faith of a people is the historical construct of a particular type of culture, then those born in or raised within the United States are a product of a society where white supremacy and class privilege have been woven into the very fabric of how whites see themselves and organize the world around them. My colleague Kelly Brown Douglas reminds us that the language of "exceptionalism," which is partially responsible for Trump's victory, can be traced back to the Pilgrims and Puritans who fled Europe in search of religious freedom. Before the conquest of what would eventually become the United States of America, these early invaders saw themselves as descendants of an ancient, superior Anglo-Saxon race "free from the taint of intermarriages with foreign nations." *Germania*, written by the Roman historian Publius Cornelius Tacitus in 98 CE, described a people who were brave, faithful, virtuous, and honorable. Their racial purity, he wrote, contributed to their higher moral values and an "instinctive love for freedom." Their Teutonic descendants would cross the Atlantic—as "new Israelites"—on a divine mission to build a new religious nation true to their "exceptional" Anglo-Saxon heritage. They were destined to become the "shining light upon the hill."

This understanding of their exceptionalism was foundational in the thinking of the Founding Fathers as they established the new republic. They saw their revolution as an Anglocentric divine call. But after the end of slavery, non-Anglo-Saxon European immigrants began to arrive at these shores in large numbers. As long as they were European, close to the white Anglo-Saxon ideal, they too could learn how to be white "within the space of two generations," according to President Theodore Roosevelt. Whiteness (unattainable to non-Europeans) became the passport into the exceptional space we have come to call America. But as nonwhites began to demand their human rights during the 1960s and began to make strides in creating a more just social arrangement, the guardians of white exceptionalism perceived the danger of diluting their supposed supremacy. As repugnant as miscegenation, illegal until 1967, may have been for them, even worse would be the notion of nonwhites occupying exceptional white spaces—like the appropriately named White House.

Although institutional racism did not abate, its historical enforcers began to be seen as politically incorrect. Modern racism required sophistication, thus making race-based groups like neo-Nazis, skinheads, and the Klan embarrassments. During the last decades of the twentieth century, members of those groups were dismissed as yokels by educated people who understood critical "race theory." However, the benign act of dismissing those hate groups as irrelevant hid the fact that racism was alive and well, and had not, in fact, ended or lost its potency. This also meant white Christian nationalists—clinging to feelings of exceptionalism and superiority—had, in fact, mastered political correctness. During this time, avowed racist groups were no longer taken seriously and were even relegated to the status of ignorant rabble-rousers, until Trump capitalized on their humiliation and ostracization. Through coded (and at times not-so-coded) language, political speeches stoked the cravings of "the forgotten Americans" for their nation to return to its past glories. For them, America, a once proud nation, had lost her way and had journeyed far from her mystical origins. Trump's inaugural address, which claimed to expose the truth of a dark and divided America, issued a call to stop such "American carnage . . . right here and right now." Trump's genius is the simplicity of his message: Make America Great Again, where "great" gets to be defined in whatever matter the hearer, specifically the racist hearer, wishes to define the term. Even if some of Trump's other pronouncements appeared obscene or obnoxious to his devotees, moral objections could be set aside for the reestablishment of a supremacy deemed lost.

Celebrating Trump for his fearlessness and speaking his mind—that is, being unashamedly racist in his description of citizens of color—these racist groups, previously ignored, experienced an invigorating resurgence. It has never been a secret that rabid white supremacists such as David Duke support Trump, as do hate groups such as the ones who marched in Charlottesville. And yet Trump refused to disavow such groups in the wake of the violence they perpetrated until he was forced to do so days later in the face of mounting pressure and criticism. Was anyone really fooled by his delayed indignation, which should have occurred immediately? When a pair of Massachusetts men in August 2015 beat a homeless Latino whom they had encountered on the streets with a pipe yelling, "Donald Trump is right;" the then-candidate said it was a shame—before praising the passion of his followers: "They love this country, they want this country to be great again." Days later, and only after facing mounting criticism, he condemned the violence.[3]

These historical racist and classist national underpinnings contribute to the creation of a religious metanarrative that justifies and protects the dominant culture and those whom the culture was designed to privilege. A so-called Christian worldview is created where complicity with the imperial imagination of the United States is deemed normal and where those who benefit by God and country usually accept the present order of things, failing to consider the depths and pervasiveness of the racialization of their faith. Few white Christians, and Christians of color seeking salvation through assimilation, recognize how the Christianity they advocate is reinforced and privileged by economic class and whiteness. As alluring as Eurocentric Christianity with its simplistic solutions to life's complexities may appear to be for the dispossessed, most of this form of Christianity remains embedded within whiteness and is thus incongruent with the gospel message of liberation.

Because social order in the United States continues to thrive on injustice, a national faith must be created that neither threatens or challenges the status quo. Calls for justice are either dismissed as a utopian vision that can never be realized until Jesus's second coming (Billy Graham), seen as the antithesis of faith requiring true believers to flee from churches advocating social or economic justice (Glenn Beck), or described as a mistake made by the church, which should instead concentrate on simply being the church, living within the faith community as if Christ's message is true (Stanley Hauerwas). The problem with white Christianity is that most Christian moral reasoning is done from the sectarian realm of abstractions. Christianity has a problem with "what you do" because of its focus on "how you believe." A mental decision to accept Jesus Christ as one's Lord and savior trumps using Jesus Christ as the paradigm for how to live one's life.

Through this sleight of hand, white Christians can profess their belief in Jesus while refusing to "be Jesus" and create a more just social order, or worse, can engage in activities diametrically opposed to Jesus's life and teachings. How else can Christians called to having their yea be yea support a pathological liar who made 2,140 false or misleading claims during his first year in office (or about six a day), according to the *Washington Post* fact checker?[4] How else can Christians advocating family values dismiss the trysts of a serial adulterer who calls for the separation of immigrant children from their parents? How else can Christians who insist on pietist virtues and values support Dennis Hof, a pimp and owner of several bordellos, as candidate for the Nevada legislature? How else can Christians called to feed the hungry, give drink to the thirsty, and clothe the naked encourage the dismantling of the minimal United States safety net that provided bare scraps of humanity and whose absence will cause unbearable misery when the next recession hits? Christians in the United States embrace untruthfulness, infidelity, and selfish greed as long as they advance conservative political and economic ideologies. The problem with whiteness is that the Christianity it advocates is, has been, and will always be idolatrous.

And while it is true that some white Christians might lean toward a more praxis-oriented faith, a commitment to abstract thinking over actively living one's faith dominates the Euro-American Christian milieu. Why then should people of color assimilate to a white Christianity that dismisses the justice we call for and demands replacing praxis with ethereal thoughts? For the disenfranchised to assimilate to the white Christianity of either conservatives or liberals is damning, if not deadly, to our very existential being, even when Christianity is repackaged as progressive and worthy of implementation for marginalized communities. This driving force responsible for electing authoritarian figures who privilege whiteness at the expense of others is a Eurocentric-driven problem creating a culture where communities of color are the object and the problem, never the subject or the solution. In order to reconcile the whiteness that benefits them with their commitment to Christianity, the dominant Euro-American culture must have an abstract faith that, while distinctly Eurocentric, can be presented as universal. And while Christianity in the United States is neither uniform nor monolithic, still certain common denominators exist, such as a propensity toward hyperindividualism, a call for law and order, an emphasis on charity over and against justice, an uncritical acceptance of the market economy, an emphasis on whiteness, and prominent patriarchal structural norms. While such a Christianity is compatible with the dominant Euro-American culture, it remains incongruent for those residing on the margins of society because of how such a faith reinforces the prevailing social structures responsible for the causes of disenfranchisement.

The problem with whiteness is not a new concern; its roots can be traced to the so-called Age of Enlightenment, which spurred the development of racial classifications. Eurocentric enlightenment thought was obsessed with categorizing nature for the purpose of easy possession. Among those categorized by museums and scholars were people groups. Preoccupation with defining race through evolutionary stages became foundational in the intellectual justification for the imperial conquest and slavery of those supposedly stuck at the lower stages of evolution. And while the modernity project attempted to replace God with science, Christianity nevertheless played a crucial role in globalizing racist practices. White Christians, using biblical justifications (the sin of Cain or the sin of Ham) and/or scientific justification (eugenics), were quick to describe those awaiting colonization as shiftless, lazy, childlike, dangerous, and animalistic.

This view of nonwhites was interwoven into the very fabric of Euro-American culture, becoming the foundation on which history was constructed and the norm by which it is interpreted. Racism and ethnic discrimination cease to be a matter of beliefs or intentions, becoming instead the consequences of what it means to be white. Racial definitions undergird privileges for those closest to the white ideal while disenfranchising those further away, who are relegated to live under poorer economic conditions with fewer opportunities for proper sanitation, health care, and education, all resulting in their shorter life spans. For the past five hundred years of North American history, the overwhelming majority of liberal and conservative whites saw the abnormality of racial and economic oppressions by the dominant culture as normal and legitimate, justified morally and legally.

Under His Eye

When white Christian nationalists gaze upon the bodies of those whom they define as inferior, dangerous, or impure, what do they see? For to "see" defines the existential self of the object being gazed upon. To *see* implies a position of authority, a privileged point of view. *Seeing* is not some mere physical phenomenon involving the transmission of light waves. Seeing encompasses more than simply transforming the image of the object focused upon by our cornea into electrical impulses carried by the optic nerve to our brain. To *see* nonwhite bodies is more than our brains simply recognizing an image, because the act of seeing conveys normalized concepts and definitions that reinforce white supremacy with every glance. *Seeing* provides sole legitimacy to a mode of thought that radically transforms the object from merely being seen into an object to be possessed and manipulated.

But defining and possessing the object first requires defining the self through the negation of the object gazed upon. Simply stated, whiteness is defined as the negation of color. For centuries, white culture has defined people of color as lazy, dangerous, and immoral. Compare how the Merriam-Webster dictionary defines black ("dirty, soiled, absence of light, sad, gloomy, calamitous, hostility, angry, discontent") with the so-called objective definition for white ("free from blemish, free from moral impurity, innocent, favorable, fortunate"). Even though more people of color have historically died at the hands of white terrorists through lynchings, race riots, and stand-your-ground legislation, white people lock their car doors when driving through black and brown neighborhoods. This is why I personally lock my doors when driving through white middle-class neighborhoods! No matter how many bow ties I may wear in a vain attempt to appear intellectually respectable, whites still see me and thus define me as a lazy, dangerous, and immoral sp*c.

Is there a quality of laziness assigned to the color black or the color brown? Is there an inherent danger found in these colors? Or is there an essential immorality associated with any of the colors of the spectrum derived from light dispersed by a prism? Color—whether it be brown, purple, orange, or blue –has no essential quality. Defining any color by applying signification to it, according to linguist Ferdinand de Saussure, is an arbitrary act. There is nothing essentially dangerous or inherently immoral about the colors black, white, green, or even magenta. Cultures link and naturalize the signified "danger" (mental concept) with the signifier "black" (material aspect). There is no reason whatsoever why the signifier "black" or "brown" engenders the signified. And yet, these definitions, as cultural norms, arbitrarily link black and brown bodies to ideas such as lazy, dangerous, and immoral—making them appear to be necessary and indisputably entrenched facts. The concepts of "blackish" and "brownish" become antisocial qualities rather than simply two colors of a rainbow. The words used to define communities of color—used "objectively" by dictionaries—were socially constructed not to be descriptive but prescriptive, with the power of their connotations invoking action. The words chosen to signify what is seen are a product of a white, Christian, nationalist society determined to perpetuate white supremacy as normal, legitimate, and natural.

Power is conveyed to the one who sees. White Christians understand who they are when they tell themselves *who they are not*. They self-define as subjects by contrasting themselves with the object they see, an object that defines what it means to be white by emphasizing the differences with the other. This act of seeing establishes nationwide power relations that define how members of the dominant culture see themselves and how they impose a definition on nonwhites. When Christian whites look at themselves in Lacan's mirror, they do not see a black or a brown person, defined—as we are reminded by objective dictionaries—as being lazy, dangerous, and immoral. "Black people are lazy. I don't see a black person in the mirror's reflection; therefore, I'm industrious. Brown people are dangerous. I don't see a brown person in the mirror's reflection; therefore, I'm harmless. Black and brown people are immoral. I don't see a black or brown person in the mirror's reflection; therefore, I'm a virtuous, God-fearing Christian."

White Christian vices and desires are projected upon darker bodies. Before the Christian white's subjective "I," all others occupy the space "I am not." Both Christians in the United States and those upon whom they gaze are entangled and intertwined because of the unwanted and unwelcome sodomizing of the mind caused by the white gaze. For theological reflection to be relevant, the identity of this "I am not," constructed by the dominant "I," must be debunked. Exposing the social fabrication of the "I" disrupts the prevailing normalization of distinctions and unveils the hidden dynamics of oppression. A major problem facing marginalized communities is that since childhood they have been taught to see and interpret reality through the eyes of the dominant culture. The triumph of the colonizing process is best demonstrated when people of color define themselves and their communities through white, Christian paradigms, which consciously or unconsciously contribute to their marginalization. Decoloniality begins when the gazed-upon attempt to see themselves with their own eyes.

White Victimhood

Why do those who control all the levers of power in the United States, the government, the military, the boardrooms, and the religious institutions constantly *see* and portray themselves as victims? This strategy of oppressors attempting to appear as though they are oppressed wields tremendous power. The church of white Christianity, Fox News, preaches this falsehood in their enduring effort to destabilize truth. Candles continue to be lit to their martyred Saint O'Reilly by Cardinals Tucker Carlson and Sean Hannity as they perpetuate the illusion of a Christianity under siege, a church under attack. Come December, reports of a war on Christmas will permeate their airwaves. Their mental contortions to falsify reality would make a Kama Sutra expert blush. By creating their imaginary victimhood, white Christians construct the platform from which political saviors can manipulate these faithful by offering a false security rooted in the illusion of white privilege. They mask their racism by finding faces of color who rack up six-figure incomes to offer prayers during inaugural rituals of a misogynist racist. They preach a false, flimsy, and futile Christianity, one committed more to mammon and Caesar than to the poor, homeless, undocumented, and dark-skinned Middle Eastern born in a stable and crucified on a cross.

For years I have written of my hopelessness in the face of institutional racism and ethnic discrimination masked by liberal friends who spoke about a post-racial America because they voted for a black man. With the election of Donald Trump the true face of this country has been unveiled, and I am terrified—terrified of what I see, terrified for my economic and physical safety and for that of my children. I am terrified of white Christians who stood in solidarity with white supremacists to elect a man promising to take their country back. But what is missing from such slogans is *from whom* are they taking the country back? The threat preventing them from enjoying domestic tranquility are the "colors"—rapist Mexicans crossing the borders or oversexed black bucks living off welfare. The threat preventing peace of mind is a political correctness that castigates whites for being as publically racist and sexist as they want to be. The threat preventing participating in the general welfare is those damn illegals and affirmative action recipients taking away jobs belonging to true, red-blooded Americans—in other words, whites. It never ceases to amaze me that those who are most privileged by society's standards, whose paychecks, when compared to those of people of color, are substantially higher for doing the same jobs, who are the first hired and last fired, tend to rewrite themselves into the national narrative as victims.

Recasting oneself as a victim liberates the victimizer from having to deal with how societal structure has been normalized to privilege them. Only whites "belong" in the United States, others simply live here. And as guests, these others should learn how to hold their tongues, for whenever they dare to demand treatment as equal citizens, Euro-Americans feign victimhood for being held responsible for their racism. To describe, as I am, how communities of color are disenfranchised is to welcome accusations of being "race hustlers." Those who unmask oppressive, racist social structures give those who have historically benefited from white supremacy an excuse to cast themselves as living under a tyranny of political correctness established by haters of whites who seek to blame Euro-Americans for all of their problems. As a response to this colored threat, they advocate the passage of laws dressed as the protection of religious liberties that actually mask bigotry against those who seek to be accepted as fellow humans and citizens.

And yet, whites are indeed victims in one way. They too are victims of the very structures designed to protect their power and privilege. Because racism and ethnic discrimination are woven into the history of the United States, everyone, including whites, is taught their place in society and how they should relate to one another. Since childhood, we who reside on the underside of history have been taught to see and interpret reality through the white, Christian eyes of the dominant culture, specifically through middle-upper-class, cis-male, patriarchal eyes. Most communities teach the "white" norm as the legitimate way to interact with others. Teaching this norm forces children to suppress their natural inclinations to play and relate with each other at daycare or school. In kindergarten children naturally play together, regardless of race or gender, but by the time they reach high school they have all been taught and conditioned to sit at different tables in the school cafeteria. They learn to mistrust their co-students because they fear being exiled from their own community. "You better not date a Latino man or I'll disown you," a parent may verbally or nonverbally communicate to a daughter. Or children may learn to remain silent or only giggle nervously in response to racist jokes, slurs, or abuses.

Euro-Americans, seeing themselves as the norm, are, in effect, without race. That is, everyone else is "colored," while they, as whites, have no color. For example, members of the dominant culture refer to the black cop, the Hispanic teacher, or the Asian mechanic. Seldom do they refer to the white cop, the white teacher, or the white mechanic, mostly because the norm of whiteness makes everyone white unless otherwise noted. Yet, when children reach adulthood, they must begin to deal with the contradictory racial statements, emotions, and mental states that arise when they try to reconcile the need to belong to their group with how they are taught to deal with those of other groups. Obviously, oppressed-oppressor dichotomies are too simplistic to be helpful in the quest for a more liberating, just society. And while we should avoid equating the harm white supremacy does to Euro-Americans with what it does to those on their margins, still we should recognize that those who benefit from a society structured to privilege them due to skin pigmentation are also abused by those same structures. They too are indoctrinated to believe they deserve, or earn, or have a right to disproportionate power and privilege. They are trapped into living up to the false ideal of superiority and as such require the same liberation yearned for by the disenfranchised. Liberation from death-dealing social structures is both for the abused that are denied their humanity; and for their abusers whose own humanity is lost through their complicity with these same structures. The horrors faced at the hands of fellow humans have more to do with white ignorance than any particular character flaw. White Christian ignorance is learned and legitimized, becoming normative within a society based on hatred.

But hate must be answered with love. As an act of love, we must tear Christ from the hands of these white Christians whose hearts beat callous and stony within their chests—a love that pities but does not hate. To hate is to vilify those whose own ignorance makes them complicit with one's oppression. I refuse to hate. I refuse to make those who are benefiting from my oppression into monsters. To hate monsters justifies all the violence they deserve because they are, after all, such monsters. But rather than creating enemies to hate, I choose to see whites, those who have chosen the false narrative of a nationalist Christianity, in need of pity. The complexity of being human holds in tension loving, tender, caring individuals who nonetheless engage in satanic acts, manifested as unspeakable brutality toward fellow human beings, especially human beings of a different hue. It is so easy and so satisfying to construct enemies, and yet there are those who know exactly what they are doing when they benefit from prevailing oppressions. A nonviolent love may not lead us to a more just world, but it will contribute to a more wholesome soul. I choose to pity instead of hate for the sake of my own sanity, my own well-being, my own self-preservation, and my own Christian faith. I choose love even though I do not believe in nonviolence. The words of Cesar Chavez truly resonate with me: "I am not a nonviolent man, I am a violent man trying to be nonviolent."

Our first act of love should be to reject Eurocentric Christianity in the many forms it has taken. And out of an act of love, we should evangelize those still mired in the sin of this nationalist Christianity with the hope that they will repent and turn from their oppressive and evil ways. Liberation from the sin of white Christianity requires consciousness-raising.

The process of bringing salvation to an apostate nation whose original sin is rooted in white supremacy begins with the crucial step of clearly elucidating the fallacy of whiteness and participating in killing the white God of nationalism.

Some Gods Are Better Off Dead

The German philosopher Friedrich Nietzsche made the scandalous proclamation that "God is dead." The church's initial reaction was condemnation. But what Nietzsche actually said was: "We have killed him—you and I. All of us are his murderers. . . . God is dead. God remains dead. And we have killed him."[5] Interesting that Nietzsche did not proclaim God does not exist, but rather, this God, whom we claim exists, has been murdered by those making the claim. For Nietzsche, what was important was not God's existence, but our complicity with God's death, a necessary death if we wanted to enjoy the full sweet and juicy fruits of modernity. The death of God is necessary to avoid the obvious contradictions of those claiming Christianity while rejecting all Jesus did and commanded his disciples to do. God may very well be dead, killed by an exceptional people posing as a shining light, but it behooves the disenfranchised to ask: "Which God is dead?" And more importantly, "Which God is replacing the one killed?"

The Eurocentric modernity project, the so-called Age of Enlightenment, of replacing God with science and reason, has succeeded in giving birth to a God created in its own image, a God who became foundational in the rationalization of necessary murderous and oppressive acts required for the establishment of the global empire of the United States. Such a God has been used to justify what Nietzsche called "master morality," practiced today by nationalist Euro-American Christians because it encourages power, freedom, and strength. From this God followed an ethical discourse that might challenge humanity to be compassionate (recall George W. Bush's compassionate conservatism), yet seldom challenges the structures that caused inhumane conditions, for such a challenge would threaten the privileged space of those who embrace guts, guns, and God. We embrace patriotic sentiments of supporting our troops or ensuring no child is left behind even while passing massive tax cuts, which assure that the wealthiest segments of society are enriched at the expense of our moral rhetoric and proclamations. Yes, we have killed God, but obviously the wrong God.

The God of what Nietzsche calls "slave morality," still followed by many among the disinherited, is the God whom the dominant white Christian culture seeks to assassinate. This "slave morality" advocates forgiveness, love, and humility to be learned, practiced, and adopted by the powerful and privileged; an ethics of turning the other cheek, putting the needs of others first, and laying down one's life for another; an ethic that would prove deadly for the princes and princesses of Wall Street. To "Make America Great Again" requires killing any God who advocates a "slave morality," as did our current president, who did not become a real estate tycoon by bending his knee to the God of slaves. Fawning sycophants, posing as Christian ministers, engaged in symbolic violence when they rushed to baptize this president in the putrid waters of nationalism, thus, rendering unto Caesar the things that are God's. Killing the God of slaves, the God of the dispossessed, the God of the marginalized, and the God of the disenfranchised allows white Christianity to flourish in worshipping their own God, all the while defining themselves as Christian moral agents, a new chosen people. Ironically, it is this white God of Christianity in the United States whom we should be plotting to kill and *not* the God of the oppressed. And make no mistake, the first step in killing this white God requires the demise, the death of whiteness.

But do those relegated to the underside of America's greatness, and those formerly of the white middle-class who are rapidly joining them, really want this God of Euro-American Christianity to live? As more and more people, especially the younger generations, self-describe their religious affiliation as "none," it would appear the answer is no. Such a God is morally bankrupt, and those who march to the beat of this God have lost all moral authority to make any ethical pronouncements about anyone or anything. Those who advocate for killing the God of white supremacy do so because they reject the God who is pleased when Muslims are bombed with drones, the God who unquestionably supports the NRA as the innocents are slaughtered in our schools, the God who sanctions one-fifth of the world's population to use, misuse, and abuse 80 percent of the world's resources, the God who equates blessings with riches, the God who hates gays. All should reject this satanic God. Although the religious experience offered by the God of the United States remains crucial for many within the dominant culture, this religion remains insufficient for those yearning for salvation and liberation.

The question to be asked by those dreaming of belonging to a society that does not yet exist is not whether there is a God but whether God gives a damn about our existence. The continuation of oppressive structures forces those who suffer due to their race, class, gender, religious persuasion, or sexual orientation to wonder about the very character of a God who appears mute in the face of injustice, a deafening silence heard during the crucifixion of Jesus, and of all those who continue today to be crucified so the few who are blessed can have their power and privilege saved through the blood of all the modern-day lambs led to the slaughter. Who is this God who appears to turn God's gaze from the suffering of God's people? Maybe if, like Jacob, we choose to wrestle with this God and demand to see God's face, we might just finally hear this silent God and determine what praxis to undertake.

Proof of the existence of this God of white Christian nationalism can be found in the majority of white churches where one can see the United States flag proudly waving beside the altar. The altar of God is adulterated whenever the Stars and Stripes, or the flag of any human-made government, is placed beside it. It is blasphemy to bend one's knee to both Caesar and Christ—refusing to do this, early Christians where convicted of atheism and thrown to the lions. They were charged with atheism because they rejected the God of the empire of their time. This was a badass Christianity that refused to bend its knee to Caesar and the things that were Caesar's. If we truly wish to euthanize a Eurocentric Christianity that is currently on life support, maybe those who call themselves Christians need the badass Christianity of atheists, those willing to lose their lives or livelihoods by refusing to believe in the God of today's powers and principalities. We should stop asking whether or not God exists. After all, such propositional claims can never be scientifically or rationally proven. That is why they call it faith. Instead we should focus our attention on who this God is whose existence we claim to affirm or deny.

Some gods are better off dead than alive. God will never be found in cathedrals made of crystal but instead will be walking among those oppressed. The gods who justify the present structures of oppression are better off dead, whether they be the god of capitalism, the god of socialism, the god of militarism, the god of *pax americana*, the god of Republicans or Democrats, or the god of nationalism. All gods who bestow privilege to their chosen people based on race, class, gender, religious affiliation, or sexual orientation should die. The gods of Euro-American Christianity entice us to conform to the norms of a civil religion rather than a faith that is based on radical solidarity with those being crushed within the cruel gears of the empire. However we might decide to define salvation, it must encompass the political and social realm that moves beyond the normalized self-centered individualistic spirituality of Euro-American Christianity. Badass Christianity actively seeks the death of the dominant culture's gods so that the God of the oppressed might be incarnated among today's crucified people.

4

Badass Christianity

My colleague Vincent Harding would often say, "I am a citizen of a country that does not yet exist." I would add that the country that he envisioned is a just and compassionate country thwarted from becoming reality by a pervasive Christian nationalism that needs the final nail hammered into its coffin before we could ever hope for the resurrection of Christianity. To dream with Vincent Harding of being citizens of a country that we must bring forth is to give meaning to the abeyant and unfulfilled rhetoric concerning "liberty and justice for all." Our noble 225-year experiment with democracy—stunted by genocidal racism—has the potential of being the balm to a hurting world. Blocking our path to a country based on liberty and justice are the continued attempts of Euro-American Christians to reconcile the message of the prince of peace with a nation whose global and domestic policies have historically been more aligned with the prince of death, who revels in wars and bloodletting.

Rather than being, as Martin Luther King Jr. reminds us, "the greatest purveyor of violence in the world," this nation has the ability to replace the bullets sold globally with the ballots denied domestically and abroad. We can never be the country we dream of being as long as we continue to worship a militarism that provides more death-causing weapons to the world than any other nation, while supporting an armed force greater than the military might of the next fourteen largest nations combined. We can never be the country we dream of being as long as we continue legalizing and legitimizing voter suppression, dismissing the voices of those whom this country has historically attempted to silence through electoral colleges, gerrymandering, and roll-scrubbing, and demanding photo identification cards while at the same time closing the Department of Motor Vehicles offices in minority neighborhoods.

Let us dream of a new nation by awakening from the nightmare of the nation in which we currently live—a nation that Euro-American Christianity christened as supposedly holy and pleasing to the Lord. Questioning the goodness of the United States can be deplorable and unpatriotic. But whenever patriotism replaces justice, we are in mortal danger of idolatry. If we believe the United States can be a force for good in the world, then the ultimate act of patriotism is to confront and challenge the country's current grievous race-based sins by demanding it lives up to the rhetoric it avows. True patriotism is proved by the tangible, transformative actions its citizens take to bring forth a justice-based social order. This yet-to-exist country upon which we place our hopes of one day being citizens will never come into being as long as it continues to embrace white Christianity with all of its racist, sexist, and imperialist manifestations. The demise of such a Christianity must be hastened, because no other global worldview has caused more death and destruction. Think of the religious wars, the crusades, and the genocides. The body count at the hands of so-called Christian conquerors outnumbers the grains of sand or the stars in the heavens. So let's permit the God of this white Christianity to bury itself.

Refusing the Ritual of Circumcision

In an age of political correctness, a time where words like "multicultural," "diversity," and "inclusion" have become chic, how can Euro-American Christianity color its racist theologies to make their God more appealing to diverse groups? Many white Christians scramble to erase centuries of exclusion by constructing all-inclusive façades, attempting to make diversity the church's new buzzword. We rush to translate three-hundred-year-old German hymns into Spanish to be sung by Latinxs. White people quickly learn Negro spirituals but fail to sway in sync to the beat. Ministers preach sermons instructing Euro-Americans why it is their Christian duty to reach out to their less fortunate "colored folk" with the gospel message of white assimilation, and churches attempt to appear culturally sensitive by scheduling Taco Tuesdays.

Some well-meaning white Christians do envision building the beloved community of which King dreamed, but they find it a difficult proposition because many whites in the United States continue to cling to institutionalized racism and ethnic discrimination. This does not mean such Christians are excluded from working toward the dream. It means that if they hope to be allies, they must participate in killing the God of white Christianity. But this work is not easy, the pitfalls are many, and the shortcuts are too tempting. It is so much easier to hold on to an impotent God while feigning inclusivity. Take for example, the great modern-day theologian Steven Colbert of the former *The Colbert Report*, who once satirically accepted applications in hopes of finding his very own "black friend." Realizing the importance of political correctness, Colbert thought it crucial to find a black friend he could display just in case he ever was accused of being a racist. He was so committed to the cause that he had to ask someone else to point out those who were black because, after all, he was "colorblind." Colbert made his point. All too often, white Christianity tries to follow Colbert's facetious lead in how to racially and ethnically diversify the church, taking similar shortcuts to make the segregated Sunday morning hour seem more inclusive. The hope of diversification has more to do with political correctness than creating the beloved community.

Although I do not question the sincerity of those Euro-Americans who wish to see their congregations better reflect the diversity of humanity, still, for many, their approach attempts to include faces of color without necessarily hearing voices of color. All too often, when white Christians wrestle with issues of inclusiveness, they simply publish a multicultural website containing token faces of color for the sake of political correctness. And if need be, such faces can always be Photoshopped. All are welcomed, as long as white Christian power structures remain intact. The underlying meaning of political correctness is inclusiveness as long as people of color first convert to whiteness and respond appreciatively to the varied translations of their respective cultures.

The early church in Acts faced a similar dilemma. They asked, must the Gentiles joining the faith first convert to Judaism, through the ritual of circumcision, before they can be considered Christians? Acts 15 records the controversy that took place at Antioch. "Unless you are circumcised in the tradition of Moses, you cannot be saved" (verse 1), cried out the guardians of the faith. Even the most faithful to God can revert back to the prejudices lurking in their hearts as exemplified by Peter, who refused to break bread with these Gentiles. This is the same Peter who was once criticized for visiting the home of the Gentile Cornelius, a Roman centurion. But while Peter was in Antioch, when certain men of Jerusalem arrived to insist Gentiles must first be circumcised before being saved, Peter did what so many whites do when threatened with being traitors to their race, *he remained silent* and did not stand in solidarity with the marginalized by sitting down and eating with the uncircumcised Gentiles.

Eventually the controversy was settled in favor of the Gentiles. They could become Christians without participating in the ritual of circumcision, that is, without first having to become Jews. Although the church decided then that non-Jews need not be circumcised, the controversy over inclusion continues to rage. Today, the Euro-American church demands not to physically cut off the foreskin of men but rather to force communities of color, both men and women, to cut off the foreskin of their identity, their culture, and the symbols by which they perceive the physical and metaphysical world. To become Christian, those whom this brand of the Christian tradition oppressed and repressed must first become white. They must adopt Euro-American theology, philosophy, liturgy, hermeneutics, politics, and most importantly, ecclesiology. Yes, they can translate hymns into their native languages or incorporate the use of some cultural symbols, but still they must prove their Christianity by describing their faith in the symbols of the dominant culture through Eurocentric philosophical and theological language, the same language used for centuries to justify oppression and to relegate nonwhites to invisibility. To insist on believing through one's own indigenous symbols only proves that—like the uncircumcised Gentiles of old—they are not *really* believers, and even if they are, they have a more primitive, uninformed, and backward faith than their Euro-American superiors.

If marginalized people wish to be baptized into the Christianity predominant in the United States, the ritual of identity-circumcision becomes their initiation to the faith, a death-causing cut deemed cheap by white Christians. Why should I come running now, after centuries of exclusion, so that the white churches can appear more hip, inclusive, and woke by having a black or brown face in the pew? While I appreciate the invitation to self-mutilate, I must ask, why do you assume I would even *want* to worship at your white church? It is difficult for people of color to worship God, whom we ask to forgive our debts, while sitting next to the banker who will charge an extra point of interest on our debt because our last names are Latinx. It's hard to pray for peace in church while the police officer who gave us tickets for driving-while-black stares at us. It's challenging to proclaim the mercies of my God when the congregant sitting across the aisle from me flaunts a "Build That Wall" political button, refusing to show mercy toward the undocumented. Unless those within Euro-American Christianity begin to deal honestly and seriously with their white supremacy and class privilege, it is unlikely believers of color will ignore the realities outside the church building and just join them. I contend that nationalist Christianity and its white theology rooted in Euro-centric philosophy are simply beyond reform, because this is what we people of color see and live every day. Rejecting this form of Christianity is, frankly, crucial to our own mental health, not to mention our physical and societal well-being.

All of us share a common history in which racial and ethnic forms of oppression have been legalized, legitimized, and normalized. Most Euro-American churches, along with circumcised communities of color, have come to religiously justify their very being within this white Christianity. Due to the Civil Rights movement of the 1960s—and other antiracist, anticolonial, and democratizing movements throughout the world—the way whites construct reality was radically challenged and changed. Nonetheless, the repackaging of white supremacy and exceptionalism was accomplished under the label of "color blindness," designed to preserve the historical racial hegemony. Claiming color blindness simply places questions concerning the struggle for justice on a universal rather than on a corporate plane by integrating the opposition so as to nullify their more radical demands. The reconciliation forged and advocated is a color-blind reconciliation that enacts antiracist laws while failing to fundamentally change or transform the social structures that maintain and sustain racism. A minority of people of color, usually with middle-class privilege, willing to self-circumcise the foreskin of their culture for the sake of profitable inclusion, often sacrifice radical demands in favor of limited economic, political, and cultural access to power and privilege.

To claim the ideal of color blindness allows white Christians to approach racism on an individual basis rather than a

communal level. Euro-Americans can downplay, if not outright ignore, the importance of initiating sociopolitical acts
that challenge the present embedded social structures. Rather
than seeking to exorcise communal racist policies from their
religious organizations, they prefer simply to ask for individual forgiveness. Reconciliation is reduced to the individual
level and is achieved through personal relationships established across racial and ethnic lines. Emphasizing individu-
al-level actions rather than changing racist social structures
allows those privileged by those same structures with whiteness to feel vindicated because public apologies were offered
for past racist acts. Meanwhile, they continue to benefit from
the status quo established to protect white privilege.

Moving beyond a façade of political correctness means
the dominant culture's consciousness must be raised to consider the struggles of their neighbors of color, while at the
same time not making members of that culture defensive.
Christianity in the United States discovers its own salvation
through its solidarity with the Christianity of the marginalized. Such Christians engage in the process of envisioning a
new reality but not simply with the goal of having more faces
of color scattered throughout white Christian churches in the
United States. Such Christians dream for the sole purpose of
becoming citizens of a country that does not yet exist. Thus
the question facing us is, what is the best advice that we can
give to whites living in a so-called post-racial society who
wish to diversify their institutions but still demand that non-

whites circumcise their identity? To paraphrase Paul's rather earthy rebuttal to those Gentiles being hounded to become circumcised so that they might be saved, "I wish that the ones causing you to doubt would castrate themselves" (Gal. 5:12).

Nuestro Vino de Plátano

If we are serious about the demise of the God of white Christianity, we should begin with making plantain wine. We are a hemiplegic nation, paralyzed by a Christianity that enables racism to flourish while at the same time dooming any hope of creating a more perfect union. When a slaveholder, who exercised his legal right to rape the female bodies he owned, penned the immortal words, "We hold these truths to be self-evident: that all men are created equal; that they are endowed by their Creator with certain unalienable rights; that among these are life, liberty, and the pursuit of happiness," he never intended to include his human property in that declaration. And at the time, no one made the mistake of thinking he did. Life, liberty, and the pursuit of happiness were exclusively for whites. Since the foundation of the republic, whites understood the rhetoric concerning freedom and equality was never meant for blacks, Indians, Asians, Latinxs, or non-Christians. The American dream was never meant to be inclusive. This American dream, reserved for only whites, could exist only if the excluded nonwhites lived the American Nightmare of genocide, land theft, slavery, Manifest Destiny, gunboat diplomacy, Jim and Jane Crow, colonial expansion, and wage exploitation.

I am convinced that all Eurocentric philosophical thought and religious movements—yes, I did say all—are oppressive and repressive to those who occupy colonized spaces. The French Revolution's battle cry for *Liberté, Egalité, Fraternité* did not include her colonies in Vietnam or Algiers. When G. W. F. Hegel attempted to establish ahistorical truths, he rooted his work on the genetic superiority of the Europeans, which led to the exclusion of inferior nonwhites. According to his 1824 book *The Philosophical History of the World*, northern Europe— specifically the German spirit—is the spirit of the new world. The movement of this spirit, characterized as the realization of absolute truth, represents the unlimited self-determination of freedom, a freedom that was never meant for those needing to be civilized and Christianized. I recognized this philosophical foundation as a small boy in first grade reciting the Pledge of Allegiance during the early 1960s in Queens, New York. Even at that young age I already understood that the rhetorical end to my daily oath of "liberty and justice for all" was never meant for me, those of African descent, or their neighbors who hail from south of the border.

The "for all" prominently expressed throughout the political and religious thought of the United States is reserved for whites, not her colonies nor those among the colonized who find themselves residing in the center of empire. But how does one reconcile white Christianity with the rhetoric of "for all"? White Christians are not hypocritical because they spew liberty and justice rhetoric; instead, they are deceived by embracing a philosophically and spiritually constructed worldview that justifies oppression through freedom-based language. White Christians understand their faith in abstract terms; at the same time, their faith is devoid and dismissive of acts of social justice. This attitude enables them to obscure the violence of disinheriting, disempowering, and dispossessing nonwhites while embracing religious sentiments.

The minds of people of color are so colonized that all too often they cling to the very Eurocentric philosophical and religious thoughts detrimental to their communities, and by extension they embrace the same social structures undergirded by the same white, abstract thought that has historically proven death-dealing to them, their families, and their communities. White power and privilege have normalized and legitimized an abstract philosophical way of thinking and a spiritual way of being that enslave the minds of the disenfranchised while providing the illusion that their bodies are free. Domesticating the minds of the marginalized liberates those who benefit by how society is constructed from worrying about "free" bodies of color resisting oppression. Colonized minds relieve the anxieties of those whom society privileges from what those falling short of the white ideal might do. Carter G. Woodson, son of African slaves and among the first to study the black experience within the United States, prob-

Badass Christianity

ably said it best, "If you make a man feel that he is inferior, you do not have to compel him to accept an inferior status, for he will seek it for himself. If you make a man think that he is justly an outcast, you do not have to order him to the back door, he will go without being told; and if there is no back door, his very nature will demand one."[1] The tragedy of faith is when brown and black bodies demand that back doors be built at white churches so they can enter on bended knees to worship the white Jesus of Euro-American Christianity.

No person can serve two masters, because that person will love one and despise the other. For those who have suffered marginalization under white supremacy to love Eurocentric philosophical and theological thought, which has always excluded them, or to worship the white Jesus who justifies their subservience, will lead them to despising the philosophical wisdom emanating from their own culture and the actual Christianity based on Jesus's teachings. Attempting to interpret Christianity through Eurocentric philosophical and theological paradigms is akin to putting their white Jesus in blackface. For Christianity to experience resurrection, Eurocentric Christianity in its nationalist garb must first be crucified. The crucifixion of white Christianity and the empire it justifies begins with its total and complete rejection. At the close of the nineteenth century, Cuban philosopher and revolutionary José Martí perceived the perils of a people relegated to the underside of the emerging North American empire. He feared Cubans would adopt the very same Eurocentric philosophical worldviews that were detrimental to their existential being. He called upon the oppressed of the world to forge a new way of being, a new way of thinking, a new way of contemplating the metaphysical grounded on their indigeneity. "*¡Nuestro vino de plátano y si es agrio, es nuestro vino!*" he wrote. For those who have yet to learn to speak the language of the angels, allow me to translate: "Let us make our wine out of plantains, and even if it turns sour, it is still our own wine!" In other words, even if our own plans and projects turn out poorly, they are still better because they are our own. Why? Because they are ours, made from our indigenous ingredients. For our survival, for our sanity, for our liberation, we must all become winemakers who harvest from our own vineyards.

But what do we do with this new wine we are making? Jesus provides some practical advice: don't pour the new wine into old, Eurocentric skins because the old, worn-out skins will burst, the wine will pour out, and the skins will be ruined. One must place new wine into fresh, indigenous skins so both can be preserved together. Not only must we develop new wines and new ways of thinking, but we also have the responsibility to create new social structures, new skins that will hold our wine. Unfortunately, our beloved inclinations toward liberation have, more often than not, looked toward our oppressors for means of defining and expressing our thoughts. We attempt to simply add some token color to white thought as we try to humanize those Eurocentric thinkers who

dehumanize us. When those of us who seek a liberation meth-
odology build upon Eurocentric philosophical paradigms, we
construct resistance on shifting sand, contributing to and
continuing our own oppression. And worse, when elucidating our resistance through Eurocentric thought, regardless as
to how loud, fearless, and passionate we may sound, we are
undermining our ability to bring about permanent change.
The difficult task before us is to think new thoughts of our
own accord, instead of as a response to Eurocentric ways and
beliefs, and to imagine a more indigenous radical worldview
different from the normative philosophies that have historically justified our subservient place within society.

Our Next Emperor

The sun will one day set on the Trump presidency. Maybe
it already has, if you are reading this under the presidential
administration of number 46. Trump will leave office and
someone else will be elected. Maybe a liberal or a progressive?
Maybe a woman of color? Or maybe another alt-right candidate? But even if a Lincoln follows a Buchanan, little will
change with the next person who occupies the office of the
presidency. We may indeed have a kinder, gentler approach
to governance, but unless we deal with the underlying causes
that gave rise to Trump in the first place, it will be only a matter of time before Trump's legacy is expanded and extended.

Trump is not the cause of oppression among those marginalized in the United States; he is merely the symptom, the mucus of a cold, the pus of an abscess, the latest manifestation of white supremacy.

Regardless of skin pigmentation, gender, or ethnic background, the leader of an empire is stilled call the emperor or empress. No one can become the leader of the world's most powerful empire if he or she is unwilling to defend what whiteness symbolizes globally. If the interests of Mobil, Microsoft, or McDonalds in penetrating open markets are ever threatened, the president—liberal or conservative—will place the full forces of the empire at these corporations' disposal, even at the expense of threatening justice, and even at the cost of committing United States troops. And if the captains of industry were ever to be threatened with an economic or political reversal of fortune, the future president, regardless of partisan politics, would rally all the forces at her or his disposal to ensure that the prevailing economic power structures would continue unhindered, even if those structures are detrimental to communities that share the same gender, skin pigmentation, or ethnicity as the emperor or empress.

Whoever succeeds Trump will pay lip service to Euro-American Christianity while defending free-market policies and ignoring the undemocratic distribution of wealth, resources, and privileges. Regardless of who follows Trump, this country's distribution of income and opportunities will still fall along racial, ethnic, and gender lines. By the time a new emperor or empress is sworn in, I predict the disparity between the rich and the poor (who are predominately people of color and female) will grow even larger than it is now, just as the gap has widened over eight years when we had a black emperor who earned the nickname "Deporter-in-Chief."

Like that of the Roman emperor of old, the task of the American leader is to secure the peace so commerce can flourish. The United States safeguards a *pax americana* so that elite business leaders within the empire, and their counterparts within the countries that the United States economically dominates, can harvest the benefits stolen from the vast majority of the world's marginalized. Modern-day empires can arise only through the existence of the foreign and domestic disenfranchised groups that are needed to provide both raw materials and cheap labor. The wealth, prosperity, and power of the center remain dependent upon the exploitation of the groups of people who exist on the global margins. Economic structures and relationships create and heavily influence societal power relationships.

Those who resided in what is commonly called the "Third World," with their enormous human and natural wealth, provided the necessary material resources at the start of the twentieth century that transformed the anemic United States into the sole superpower at the close of that same century. Non-European land, resources, and labor, which were believed to exist to enrich the center, were obtained through murder, rape, pillage, and exploitation of those who lacked military and technological superiority. Unfortunately, military or technological superiority has come to be confused with cultural, intellectual, and religious supremacy. We who claim to be liberals and progressives should hold no illusions as to what occurs in the voting booth. When the oppressed cast their votes, it is not for the candidate who will cure the ills of the country; all too often, the oppressed cast their votes for the emperor or empress who, at the end of the day, will cause the least amount of misery and oppression for the world's disenfranchised.

Badass Christianity

Shortly before being murdered, Salvadorian archbishop Oscar Romero said, "The ones who have a voice must speak for those who are voiceless." This is what it means to raise consciousness and awareness. Anyone can raise awareness from the security of privileged spaces. Liberal armchair intellectuals pontificating from the safety of ivory towers shed tears over the plight of the oppressed but fail to realize the primary goal of the intellectual is to bend the moral arc of the universe toward justice and not simply to sigh over the prevailing injustices, or worse, to embrace a solely descriptive approach to scholarship. Only cowards with multiple initials after their names preach against white Christian privilege without ever risking an iota. By contrast, badass Christianity expresses radical solidarity with the world's voiceless, regardless of personal cost.

The voiceless live in a world that privileges a white, Christian worldview calling the shots, setting the rules, and giving and taking away at whim, a world where people suffer daily at the hands of those in power. As a survival tactic, many among the voiceless seldom admit their true feelings when they are asked. As my colleague Katie Cannon reminds us, "When you live with your head in the mouth of a lion, you should hold it there gingerly." Besides, since when are those in power interested in exploring the injustices they inadvertently inflict? The question is not whether the subaltern can speak, but rather, if she does, will anyone listen? Most would be shocked and offended if the powerless dared to hold them accountable for using Christianity as the means of protecting and preserving privileged spaces. Why should we be shocked when those who have experienced a lifetime of disenfranchisement appear angry and consistently seek understanding, at the gut level, from those who have benefited from oppressive structures? Even modern customer service training requires validating the distress of the dissatisfied customer.

Public discussion of certain topics—such as those covered throughout this book—is simply not allowed. Such conversations are held only within tightly controlled environments, where deviation to criticism of white Christianity is frowned upon. The voice of the powerless is permitted to be heard only if it is expressed as a token squeak, in deference to the privileged. Although the white Christian's foot is on the neck of the marginalized, the oppressed must meekly ask,

> Good afternoon, Sir, sorry to bother you Sir. May I kindly bring it to your attention that our group is not advancing due to the foot you unintentionally placed upon our neck? Do you have a moment to discuss what we perceive to be an unfortunate situation? We would appreciate the opportunity to discuss your foot in a manner which provides you with a positive and uplifting self-understanding and enlightenment. If not, then perhaps we could schedule an appointment at your earliest convenience.

White Christianity prefers to remain ignorant or silent rather than explore how their faith is but a political ideology detrimental to the vast majority of disenfranchised communities. Don't the marginalized have a right to express how they are feeling, and in their own way? Are we going to pretend the pain of the voiceless doesn't really exist, that it will simply go away if we don't talk about it? The badass Jesus to whom the marginalized turn was one who provoked the ire of the religious leaders of his time when he ate at the same table with those who were oppressed, outcast, and untouchable. Today, we can expect those who stand in solidarity with the persecuted to be treated the same. To advocate a Christianity that stands with the oppressed is to embrace the hopelessness the oppressed experience because of Eurocentric Christian rule.

We are always in a rush to get to Easter Sunday, refusing to lament before the crucified. We are so concerned with ensuring Easter celebrations—the most extravagant Sunday of the year—that we evade and ignore Holy Saturday. The biblical call to lament is all too often spurned and shunned. Lamentation, this side of Easter, is treated as a sign of unfaithfulness. And yet, it is in the space of Holy Saturday—that space after Friday's crucifixion, and the not-yet resurrection of Easter Sunday— where the vast majority of the world's disenfranchised exists. Some faint anticipation of Sunday's good news may be present, but this hope is drowned out by the reality of Friday's brutality, gore, abandonment, and violence. In this space, hopelessness becomes the companion of used, misused, and abused people. The audacity of hope becomes either the class privilege that protects the chosen from the realities of Friday or the opium used by the poor to numb the pain of oppression until Sunday's good news. Regardless of the hope we profess, the disinherited, along with their children and their children's children, will more than likely continue to live in abject poverty caused so that the frozen chosen can economically benefit and enjoy a sumptuous spread during Easter brunch. Sunday is simply too distant and will never arrive as long as nationalist Christianity exists. No wonder I'm so hopeless.

And yet Euro-American Christianity dismisses hopelessness in exchange for an oppressive optimism that ignores the world where eight men (Bill Gates, Amancio Ortega, Warren Buffett, Carlos Slim, Jeff Bezos, Mark Zuckerberg, Larry Ellison, and Michael Bloomberg) are wealthier than half of humanity. Rather than looking up at those who benefit from this new global neoliberal model, we blame the poor, the immigrant, and the persons of color. Assurances that hope will prevail might temporarily soothe one's anxieties, but they fall short of bringing forth a more just economic social structure that is not based on the marginalization of those already tormented by economic suffering.

Insisting on hope gets in the way of listening and learning from the oppressed. This hopelessness that I advocate is not despair but desperation. Despair puts one in a fetal position where all one does is wail and gnash his or her teeth. Desperation propels one toward concrete actions, because there is nothing left to lose. And when the oppressed realize they have nothing to lose, they are the most dangerous, overturning societal structures of oppression. Hope is trusting and believing that the arc of the moral universe bends toward justice, as Martin Luther King Jr. reminded us. But if we let the past and present be our guides, the existence of such an arc is nothing but a faith statement assumed without proof. In reality, the moral universe does not care, since it bends toward justice as much as it does toward oppression. If we expect this moral universal arc to bend at all toward justice, then it is up to us to do the bending.

Hope, as an unfounded statement of belief, serves an important economic purpose, becoming an excuse not to deal with the reality of injustice. I began to develop this theology of hopelessness while visiting the squatter villages of Cuernavaca, Mexico, with a group of predominately white, liberal Christian students. We were going to the poor to learn economic truths from them. We spent time listening to the stories of families living in life-denying poverty. That evening, as we unpacked what we saw and heard, one of my white students stated that, in spite of the horrific conditions she had witnessed, she still saw "the hope in the eyes of the little girls." Hearing her excuse for these conditions made me suffer an epistemological breakdown. I immediately responded that these same little girls on whom she is imposing First World hope would be, within a decade, selling their bodies or trapped in abusive marriages to put food on the table; hence, I wasn't sure what kind of hope my student saw in their eyes. Among the marginalized, the disadvantaged, the least of the least, I discovered an ethos where hope is not necessarily apparent. Since then, I have come to realize that for many of the wretched of the earth, hope is mainly claimed by white Christians with economic privilege, serving as a means of distancing themselves from the unsolvable disenfranchisement most of the world's poor are forced to face.

If indeed all faith traditions are contextual, then the "decent" Christianity whites advocate will remain incongruent with the survival ethics the disenfranchised need. They need a vulgar and indecent ethics shaped by the conditions marginalized communities are forced to endure. The marginalized require a subversive and disruptive Christianity that decenters normative, nationalist Christianity and its legitimization of the dominant bourgeois lifestyle. White Christianity fails the oppressed when it refuses to contemplate how empire is essentially a Eurocentric problem—a problem white Christianity aids and abets.

Simply stated, Christianity in the United States will not save the marginalized, mainly because they remain invisible and ignored. Euro-American Christianity is not for them, but it has fooled them into believing it is. For Christianity to be liberating, to be badass, it must move beyond the decent Christianity of the empire. Why? Because the prevalent Christianity of the United States was established on providing justification for the prevailing structures of oppression detrimental to people of color. The failure of Euro-American Christianity to address oppressive structures means we are left with no other choice but to envision new paradigms for marginalized communities, paradigms rooted within their context. Those who benefit from the power and privilege accorded by the dominant culture are incapable of fashioning an objective faith-based response because their standing within society is protected by the prevailing social structures. Whites who chose to become liberated must also move away from their white Christianity and join in solidarity with marginalized communities in order to participate in liberating praxis—that is, they must take actions rooted in the social location of the marginalized. This is because any faith that claims to be Christian and yet is divorced from action is irrelevant and erroneous. In short, whites seeking salvation must become traitors to their own race and class—if not, they remain forever damned.

Disenfranchised communities need to embrace a badass Christianity that rejects the predominant Christian nationalism of the empire. What is this badass Christianity? Badass Christianity is

- the decolonization of a liberating faith expression intended to upset the prevailing social order designed to maintain neoliberalism.
- a commitment to a radical solidary with the oppressed, realizing that no one can ever be "saved" as long as the poor continue to be damned by our current economic structures.
- a celebration of belief through whichever cultural symbols best connect us to the Deity.
- a rejection of laws and regulations made mainly by men, specifically white men, which trespass upon the basic rights of all.
- a survival ethics that responds to the hopelessness of the people.
- a liberation and salvation discovered as one struggles with others for the liberation of all.
- a rejection of Eurocentric theological thought due to its colonizing, philosophical world view.

- disruptive and revolutionary, overturning the temple's tables of oppressors.
- calling bullsh*t on religious and political hypocrisy.
- costly—sacrificing all, even one's life or security, for the sake of justice.

Such a Christianity can arise only from the margins of society among those who are disenchanted, disheartened, and discouraged with the normative and subjective Eurocentric virtues expounded in Euro-American Christianity. While white Christianity insists on law and order, where protest is permissible as long as it does not upset societal equilibrium, marginalized communities must call for disruption and social disorder. Instability might lead some within the dominant culture to occupy the same hopelessness-space of those unable to overcome neoliberal global forces. Such uncertainty may very well be the only way to make progress. Such a bad-ass Christianity can be frightening to those accustomed to their power and privilege, because hopelessness is equated with lacking control. Those accustomed to the benefits provided by the present social structures insist on control lest what they have be jeopardized. Sharing the plight of being vulnerable to forces beyond one's control demonstrates hope's shortcomings. And here lies the paradox: hope exists only if it is first crucified and then, maybe, resurrected.

This badass Christian approach moves toward a subversive and radical response to oppressive structures, for it refuses to play by the rules established by those who made the rules—rules that provide space only for orderly dissent, pacifying the need to protest but designed not to threaten or endanger the prevailing power relationships. Protest has been so domesticated that we must go to the police department to obtain a permit to picket the police department for the brutality of the police department. Law and order become the ethical norms whites imposed on repressed, disenfranchised communities without ever needing to ponder whose law and what order is being demanded. We have the freedom to protest, as long as it does not disrupt or endanger the social equilibrium demanded by those whom society privileges. For the disinherited, the disenfranchised, and the dispossessed to radically challenge the prevailing status quo, they must adhere to a badass Christianity, which has no qualms with overturning banker's tables—just as Jesus did in the temple. If the Christian goal is the transformation of ungodly social structures, then faith propels rule-breakers to challenge the dominant culture, which is charged with protecting those same structures with rules, by pushing beyond white experiences, which are normalized and legitimized as objective experiences for everyone.

Badass Christianity is one that disturbs, disrupts, and literally *screws* with the structures of oppression as a valid alternative when repression limits ethical responses. I have coined the phrase, "an ethics *para joder*" to describe this "screwing with the social structures." For those of you who have not yet mastered the linguistic dexterity to sing in multiple languages, allow me to again translate. To *joder* is the Spanish verb form of a word one never uses in polite conversation. To *joder* is "to f*ck with." The word connotes someone who purposely attempts to be a pain in the rear end, purposely causing trouble by playing the role of the trickster, who constantly disrupts the established norm to reveal bad faith and hypocrisy, who shouts from the mountain top the secrets that exclude, who audaciously refuses to stay in an assigned space. While I agree that one does not need to be profane to be profound, still, what is truly profane is not the word I am using but centuries of oppressive, death-dealing conditions those living on the margins of whiteness have been forced to endure.

An ethics *para joder* is an ethics that unapologetically and unashamedly "screws" with the prevailing power structures; it is the ethics of a badass Christianity. The disenfranchised, who stand before an entrenched Christian nationalism designed to marginalize those who fall outside of the white ideal, have few alternatives. Yes, we can always hope some white Christians might see the light and nail their power and privilege to the old rugged cross. However, millennia of history clearly indicate that the few who benefit greatly due to their power and privilege might engage in justice rhetoric but will not lift a finger to reorder society toward justice. Regardless of the good intentions of some within white Christianity, or the acts employed to paternalistically save and rescue those they see as the unfortunate (as if luck has anything to do with oppressive social structures), the devastating consequences of the Christian nationalism they adhere to are only worsening the situation as the few get wealthier and the many sink deeper into the despair of stomach-wrenching poverty. The dominant culture, including liberals and progressives, may be willing to offer charity and maybe even *drive* to a march, but few are willing or able to take a serious and implicating role in dismantling the very global structures designed to privilege them at the expense of others.

When the disenfranchised start to *joder*, it literally creates instability. Badass Christianity, which upsets the prevailing apple cart needed to maintain empire, is an ethical response arising from those on the margins of society who are disillusioned and disturbed with US Christian values and virtues. While most Euro-Americans insist social order is paramount to any ethical response to oppressive structure, marginalized communities must call for social disorder, a process achieved by *jodiendo*. A badass Christianity that encourages *jodiendo* refuses to play by the rules established by those who wrote the rules in the first place to silence dissent. Yes, the rule-makers roped off and made available a space so that those who need to vent politically can do so; however, the purpose of this assigned space is not to change or challenge the power relationships within existing social structures.

The Altar Call

The Spirit of the Lord is upon me, as the dew upon the grass early in the morning. The Spirit of the living God has called me to proclaim from the rooftops, from the mountaintops, how the innocent are being devoured by Eurocentric ministers masked as the lions of hatred and wolves of bigotry, self-appointed as the voice of God. More interested with the fullness of the collection plate than the emptiness of white congregants' souls, they preach a gospel antithetical to the liberation Jesus promised: that all might have life, and life more abundantly. These false nationalist prophets have led me to question my faith. It is difficult to have faith when the prevailing image of Christianity is hatred, anger, exclusion, and intolerance. I hang on to faith by my fingertips, refusing to confuse Christianity with the alt-right political agenda. Like so many Christians refusing to play the personal piety game of a dying faith tradition, I too no longer want or wish to be associated with an ideology responsible for tearing humanity asunder. For this reason, I have been turning my attention to a Christianity that is badass—badass enough to be distinguished from and a challenge to the dying Christian nationalism.

Only a cocksure clod would dismiss the very humanity and culture of would-be proselytes by attempting to convert them to a white, supremacist Christianity. If you are a white Christian, your salvation depends on nailing your whiteness to the cross. If you are a Christian of color, your salvation depends on nailing your white-colonized mind to the cross. Both acts are badass. I have no idea what a badass Islam, or a badass Hinduism, or a badass humanism, or a badass Buddhism looks like. Although I am certain such belief systems exist, I lack the hubris to imagine one. I'll let my sisters and brothers in those traditions figure it out, and I am looking forward to future conversation with them so I can learn how to better live my own faith. My altar call is only for those within my own Christian tradition. With every head bowed, and every heart open, as Miss Ernestine softly plays on the piano *Just as I Am*, I lift up this come-to-Jesus moment, to walk down the proverbial sawdust aisle in response to a radical call to reject the idolatry of Eurocentric Christianity and resurrect the badass Christianity Jesus modeled.

Salvation is not an abstract concept, nor an acceptance of Jesus, nor a personal warm, fuzzy feeling. It is a state of being which encompasses rescue and deliverance. White Christianity ignores the fact that both the Hebrew and Greek words for "save" connote "liberate." Etymologically, to be saved is to be liberated. Justice occurs when we are saved/liberated from sin, when sin is understood as the forces (individual and corporate) that bring oppression, enslavement, and death. To be liberated from this type of sin is to be saved. Salvation thus means more than simply acknowledging Jesus died for our sins, where salvation is obtained through right beliefs—orthodoxy. Even James, the brother of Jesus, reminds us that "the demons also believe, and tremble" (James 2:19).

But it's not just the demons who believe. White Christians like Dobson, Falwell, Perkins, and Graham, prospering from the power and privilege they have obtained at the expense of the disenfranchised, also believe and tremble at God's name. Salvation/liberation does not come about by having the right beliefs, doctrines, or ideologies, as they might argue. The emphasis of badass Christianity is not on what doctrines one accepts to obtain salvation but rather on what actions one commits that lead to communal liberation.

This salvation, understood as liberation, is for everyone: oppressed and oppressor, slave and slaveholder, subjugated and subjugator. It is for you and yours, and it is for me and mine. But while many are called, few are chosen. Jesus warns his followers to enter through the narrow gate; for wide is the gate and broad the road that leads to ruin, and many are those who enter in this fashion. But small is the gate and narrow the road that leads to life. Few find it. Euro-American Christianity with its history of oppression, enslavement, and subjugation is on the broad road that passes through the wide gate. White Christian gatekeepers prevent the many from experiencing salvation/liberation due to their complicity with social structures that bring misery to the vast majority of humanity, without regard to whatever commitment was made to Jesus or whichever sinner's prayer was recited.

How tragic that many of those who profit on the backs of the world's wretched call themselves Christians and believe they are saved because of some cultural upbringing or some intellectual (or emotional) decision to acknowledge Jesus—as if Jesus needs anyone's acknowledgment. Not everyone who calls Jesus "Lord" will enter God's reign. On the ultimate day when all must give an account, Jesus will respond, "Away from me you evildoers, for I never knew you. Only those who do the will of God will see the glories of God's reign" (Matt. 7:21-23). Badass Christianity is nothing new; it has always been an attempt to do the will of God regardless of the cost. And what, you might ask is the will of God? According to the prophet Micah it is simply: "To act with justice, to love mercy, and to walk humbly with one's God" (Mic. 6:8).

This is the day to decide. Don't be among those who are ignorant of their complicity in strengthening and expanding white privilege through their political power. Instead, choose to embrace the hopelessness caused by their actions. This does not mean giving up or curling up into a ball and doing nothing. The privileged, who can always afford to escape from reality, even if for only a moment, react to hopelessness this way. To embrace hopelessness means to accept the reality that sin, evil, and death trump our hope for utopias—especially the reality of how white hatred manifests itself among the oppressed and marginalized in destructive ways. To embrace hopelessness means to engage in survival praxis, knowing that the battle may be lost but the struggle continues because there exists no other choice but to continue struggling. To embrace hopelessness means that, regardless of how the story ends, the struggle for justice is what defines our very humanity. Yes, I am hopeless specifically because I am not surprised by the whitelash that ushered in the Trump presidency or by my white compatriots who claim color blindness while voting for one who sees color all too clearly and wishes to eradicate it in the America he plans to make great again. Sadly, I don't believe things will change—even with the election of a new president and even if the new president is liberal or progressive. I really don't. No, I will not hold hands and sing "Kumbaya" with white oppressors. Instead I ask all who seek justice, especially whites willing to repent of their complicity with white privilege, to join me in solidarity as I choose to sing a different badass song. Let us finally sing: "¡Basta!"

Notes

Chapter 1

1. Precise dates for these generations vary. Roughly, millennials were born in the early 1980s through the late 1990s; members of Generation Z were born in the late 1990s through the early 2010s.

2. "Religious Composition of Younger Millennials," *Pew Research Center: Religion & Public Life*, 2018, http://www.pewforum.org/religious-landscape-study/generational-cohort/younger-millennial/.

3. "Atheism Doubles among Generation Z," *Barna*, January 24, 2018, https://www.barna.com/research/atheism-doubles-among-generation-z/.

4. Michael Lipka and Claire Gecewicz, "More Americans Now Say They're Spiritual but Not Religious," *Pew Research Center: Religion & Public Life* (September 6, 2017): http://www.pewresearch.org/fact-tank/2017/09/06/more-americans-now-say-theyre-spiritual-but-not-religious/.

5. Gregory A. Smith and Jessica Martínez, "How the Faithful Voted: A Preliminary 2016 Analysis," *Pew Research Center: Religion & Public Life* (November 9, 2016): http://www.pewresearch.org/fact-tank/2016/11/09/how-the-faithful-voted-a-preliminary-2016-analysis/.

6. Alan Rappeport, "Donald Trump Calls Pope's Criticism 'Disgraceful.'" *The New York Times* (February 18, 2016): https://www.nytimes.com/politics/first-draft/2016/02/18/donald-trump-calls-popes-criticism-disgraceful/.

7. "Jerry Falwell Jr.: 'I Do Believe Trump Is a Christian,'" *CNN* (February 18, 2016): https://www.cnn.com/videos/tv/2016/02/18/falwell-jr-pope-using-christianity-as-criteria-for-president.cnn.

8. The author did all biblical translations (unless otherwise noted) from the original Greek or Hebrew.

9. Eugene Scott, "'You Get a Do-Over Here': Evangelical Leaders' Apparent Double-Standard on the Alleged Trump-Daniels Affair," *The Washington Post* (January 23, 2018): https://www.washingtonpost.com/news/the-fix/wp/2018/01/23/you-get-a-do-over-here-evangelical-leaders-apparent-double-standard-on-the-alleged-trump-daniels-affair/?utm_term=.e7351ab038f4.

10. Mark Silk, "A Court Evangelical Says What He Really Thinks," *Religion News Service* (May 8, 2018): https://religionnews.com/2018/05/08/a-court-evangelical-says-what-he-really-thinks/.

11. Bob Allen, "Robert Jeffress: Trump's Alleged Affair with Porn Star 'Totally Irrelevant' to His Evangelical Base," *Baptist News Global* (March 9, 2018): https://baptistnews.com/article/robert-jeffress-alleged-affair-porn-star-totally-irrelevant-trumps-evangelical-base/#.WszMZdPwbMI.

12. Sarah McCammon, "'Concerned' Evangelicals Plan to Meet with Trump as Sex Scandals Swirl," *National Public Radio* (April 6, 2018): https://www.npr.org/2018/04/06/599972396/concerned-evangelicals-plan-to-meet-with-trump-as-sex-scandals-swirl.

13. Meghan Keneally, "Trump's VP Pick Mike Pence Introduces Himself to America as 'a Christian, a Conservative and a Republican,'" *ABC News* (July 20, 2016): http://abcnews.go.com/Politics/trumps-vp-pick-mike-pence-introduces-america-christian/story?id=40756471.

14. Jason Le Miere, "Donald Trump Says 'Our Ancestors Tamed a Continent' and 'We Are Not Going to Apologize for America,'" *Newsweek* (May 25, 2018): http://www.newsweek.com/donald-trump-tame-continent-america-945121.

15. Josh Dawsey, "Trump Derides Protections for Immigrants from 'Shithole' Countries," *The Washington Post* (January 12, 2018): https://www.washingtonpost.com/politics/trump-attacks-protections-for-immigrants

-from-shithole-countries-in-oval-office-meeting/2018/01/11/bfc0725c-f711
-11e7-91af-31ac729add94_story.html?utm_term=.1b4157917ef1.

16. John Blake, "Where Billy Graham 'Missed the Mark,'" *CNN* (February 22, 2018): https://www.cnn.com/2018/02/22/us/billy-graham-mlk
-civil-rights/index.html.

17. Brian Levin and John David Reitzel, *Hate Crimes Rise in US Cities and Counties in Time of Division and Foreign Interference* (San Bernardino, CA: Center for the Study of Hate and Extremism, California State University, 2018), https://csbs.csusb.edu/sites/csusb_csbs/files/2018%20Hate%20 Report%205-141PM.pdf.

18. Nishant Kishore, et al., "Mortality in Puerto Rico after Hurricane Maria," *The New England Journal of Medicine* (May 29, 2018): https://www .nejm.org/doi/full/10.1056/NEJMsa1803972.

19. Charles Kurzman, *Muslim-American Involvement with Violent Extremism*, Chapel Hill, NC: Triangle Center on Terrorism and Homeland Security and the Police Executive Research Forum (January 18, 2019): https:// sites.duke.edu/tcths/files/2018/01/Kurzman_Muslim-American_Involve ment_with_Violent_Extremism_2017.pdf.

20. Niraj Chokshi, "Assaults Increased When Cities Hosted Trump Rallies, Study Finds," *The New York Times* (March 16, 2018): https://www .nytimes.com/2018/03/16/us/trump-rally-violence.html.

Chapter 2

1. Lee Drutman, Larry Diamond, and Joe Goldman, *Follow the Leader: Exploring American Support for Democracy and Authoritarianism* (Washington, DC: Democracy Fund Voters Study Guide, March 2018), https://www.voterstudygroup.org/publications/2017-voter-survey/follow
-the-leader.

2. Noah Bierman and Brian Bennett, "Trump Follows Up NBC Threat: 'It is frankly disgusting the way the press is able to write whatever they want to write,'" *Los Angeles Times*, October 11, 2017, http://www.la

times.com/politics/washington/la-na-pol-essential-washington-updates
-trump-follows-up-nbc-threat-it-is-1507746214-htmlstory.html.

3. Mark Berman, "Trump Tells Police Not to Worry about Injuring Suspects During Arrests," *The Washington Post*, July 28, 2017, https://www.washingtonpost.com/news/post-nation/wp/2017/07/28/trump-tells-police-not-to-worry-about-injuring-suspects-during-arrests/?utm_term=.0de6d4a1cfd3.

4. Mark Landler, "Trump Accuses Democrats of 'Treason' Amid Market Rout," *The New York Times*, February 5, 2018, https://www.nytimes.com/2018/02/05/us/politics/trump-accuses-democrats-treason-market-rout.html.

5. "Rep. Wilson Shouts, 'You Lie' to Obama During Speech," *CNN*, September 10, 2009, http://www.cnn.com/2009/POLITICS/09/09/joe.wilson/.

6. Andrew L. Whitehead, Samuel L. Perry, and Joseph O. Baker, "Make America Christian Again: Christian Nationalism and Voting for Donald Trump in the 2016 Presidential Election," *Sociology of Religion* (January 15, 2018), https://doi.org/10.1093/socrel/srx070.

7. Miguel A. De La Torre, *Doing Christian Ethics from the Margins*, 2nd ed. (Maryknoll, NY: Orbis Books, 2014), 155–59.

8. "Reconciliation Recommendations of the Senate Committee on Finance," *Congressional Budget Office Cost Estimate*, November 26, 2017, https://www.cbo.gov/system/files/115th-congress-2017-2018/costestimate/reconciliationrecommendationssfc.pdf.

9. Dwight Lyman Moody, *Moody: His Words, Work, and Workers*, ed. W. H. Daniels (New York: Nelson & Phillips, 1877), 431–32.

10. Jardine Malado, "Prosperity Preacher Jesse Duplantis Asks for Donations to Purchase $54 Million Falcon 7X Jet," *Christianity Today*, May 29, 2018, https://www.christiantoday.com/article/televangelist-jesse-duplantis-asks-followers-for-money-to-buy-new-falcon-7x-jet/129389.htm.

11. Adam Smith, *An Inquiry into the Nature and Causes of the Wealth of Nations*, Vol. I, ed. R. H. Campbell, A. S. Skinner, and W. B. Todd (Oxford, England: Clarendon Press, 1976 [1776]), 13.

12. Nichole M. Flores, "Why I Am Not a Feminist." *Women in The-*

ology (2010), http://womenintheology.org/2010/11/24/why-i-am-not-a
-feminist/.

Chapter 3

1. David Norman Smith and Eric Allen Hanley, "The Anger Games:
Who Voted for Donald Trump in the 2016 Election, and Why?" *Critical Sociology* (September 28, 2017), http://criticalsociology.org/the-anger-games
-who-voted-for-donald-trump-in-the-2016-election-and-why/.

2. Chauncey Devega, "Is Donald Trump a Cult Leader? Expert Says
He 'Fits the Stereotypical Profile,'" *Salon* (March 6, 2018), https://www.sa
lon.com/2018/03/06/is-donald-trump-a-cult-leader-expert-says-he-fits
-the-stereotypical-profile/.

3. Sara DiNatale and Maria Sacchetti, "South Boston Brothers Al-
legedly Beat Homeless Man," *Boston Globe* (August 19, 2015), https://www
.bostonglobe.com/metro/2015/08/19/homeless/iTagewS4bnvBKWxxPvF
cAJ/story.html.

4. Glenn Kessler and Meg Kelly, "President Trump Made 2,140 False
or Misleading Claims in His First Year," *The Washington Post*, January 20,
2018.

5. Friedrich Nietzsche, *The Gay Science*, ed. Bernard Williams,
trans. Josefine Nauckoff (New York: Cambridge University Press, 2001),
120.

Chapter 4

1. Carter G. Woodson, "Political Education Neglected," *The Mis-
Education of the Negro* (Mineola, NY: Dover Publications, Inc., 2005
[1933]), 55.